Move It Out!

Sharing the Mission of
Christ with Zeal

Fr. Tom Forrest, C.Ss.R.

4/26/03

FOR PATRICK AND ELIZABETH FOR
BEING SUCH CHARMING AND GENEROUS
HOST, AND FOR SHOWING ME SUCH WARM
HOSPITALITY; FROM A VERY GRATEFUL FRIEND,
Fr. Tom Forrest,

the**WORD**
among us

The Word Among Us Press
9639 Doctor Perry Road
Ijamsville, Maryland   21754
ISBN: 0-932085-99-7
www.wordamongus.org

Cover design: Christopher Ranck

Made and printed in the United States of America

Table of Contents

Preface

At the conclusion of the World Youth Day of the Great Jubilee Year 2000 in Rome, as the youth of the world were about to make their way back home, Pope John Paul II challenged them: " If you are what you should be, you will set the world ablaze."

These words come to mind when reading this latest contribution from the pen of Fr. Tom Forrest. His pen conveys all the enthusiasm that burns in his heart for the task of New Evangelization in this Third Millennium of Faith. Starting from the Universal Call to Mission and taking his cue from the first missionary of the Church today, Pope John Paul II, Fr. Tom, uses language and images that ring true to our world of today, and conveys the urgency of the mission of making Jesus known and loved. His easy manner of sharing from his personal experiences, be they from his encounters with the pope and with saintly people, be they from his own intimate relationship with Christ and his missionary journeys throughout the world, we are struck with the clarity of his message: "It is not enough that you know Jesus. You must make him known to others."

Quoting from what he calls "a startlingly beautiful Apostolic Letter entitled *On Evangelization in the Modern World*" where Pope Paul VI states: "The Church exists in order to evangelize," and drawing on the witness of the three greatest of all carriers of the Good News—John the Baptist, St. Paul and Jesus, the Word himself—Fr. Forrest sets out clear guidelines for the evangelizers of today. Intimacy with Jesus, nurtured and sustained by a constant relationship in prayer, is the only guarantee that the evangelizer will be effective. How aptly he quotes Pope John Paul II when he writes: "The missionary must be a 'contemplative in action.'"

This reminds me of what Pope Paul VI explained personally to me one day as we walked together. His Holiness, having asked me what, in my opinion, should be the most evident movements in a mature local Church, said: "The most evident movements of a mature local Church are two in number: one *ad extra*, the other *ad intra*." The urgency to go out of oneself, to proclaim the Good News *ad exteros*, combined with the need to continually return to the Source of grace and life in prayer is clearly exemplified today in the Person of Pope John Paul II, and Fr. Forrest has captured this inspired dynamic of missionary endeavor so excellently in this present work that one, on reading it, cannot but feel inspired, enthused, and truly set ablaze.

Whoever is privileged to be guided by Fr. Forrest through the pages of this truly inspired book will not fail to be inspired to respond, through the promptings of the Holy Spirit, to the Universal Call to Holiness.

Most Reverend John Magee
Bishop of Cloyne, Ireland,
and former personal secretary to the three
most recent popes

Introduction

The Universal Call to Mission

I studied my philosophy and theology in a beautiful Redemptorist seminary overlooking the Hudson River. Straight across the river a mile away was Hyde Park, summer home of the Roosevelt family. Just a little down river lay Jacques Island, believed by Jesuits to be the resting place of the North American martyrs as they made their escape from the Huron Indians of the far North.

I can remember how, on a number of occasions, I stood on the roof or glanced across the river from my seminary window to watch commuter trains gliding along the opposite bank. Restless from long years of priestly training and study lasting thirteen and a half years, I looked forward with longing to the time of ordination, when I would finally be able to share with those people rushing by on the other side of the river all the priestly services and attention that I longed to give.

Before entering the minor seminary at the age of fourteen, I and six other teenagers from the vocational club at our Brooklyn parish were interviewed by the visiting rector of the seminary. The parish priest directing our little club told us in advance the key question that would be asked, cueing us in on the expected answer. "Why do you want to become a Redemptorist priest?" would be the big question, and the required answer was: "To save my own soul and the souls of others!"

It is true that the answer was rehearsed, but it is equally true that my response was honest and accurate. I can't explain how or why, but at that early age God put this mysterious ambition in my heart: to live a holy life and to save the souls of men and women I had never met, and about whom I knew nothing more than the fact that it would be wonderful to help them get to heaven.

That was the thought I had on that seminary roof over half a century ago, watching those trains streak by at seventy miles an hour and thinking with inexplicable spiritual love how I would like to be leading those people to the peace, joy, and salvation that can be theirs forever through Jesus Christ.

The years certainly rolled by quickly, and many things in life have changed—but not everything. That early yearning must have come straight from God, because it stayed with me through the decades and is with me still.

What did change were the words and understandings with which those early hopes and youthful desires were expressed and lived. The original thoughts were focused on saving souls—my own and those of others—which, in simplest terms, meant getting all of us to the peace and joys of paradise. In time, all of this was translated into the one big word: EVANGELIZATION. It is the very same thought, of course, only now thought out a bit more completely and a little more accurately.

This deeper understanding did not come quickly, seeming to take longer than it should have. Getting others to heaven remains the ultimate and most eschatological goal, but with it now is a strong desire to lead people to the full enjoyment of the whole package of rich blessings and healings that wondrous Jesus won for us by becoming one of us and dying for us on a cross. In other words, my desire developed into the mission of proclaiming *all* of the Good News that reaches us though the incarnation, life, death, and resurrection of our Lord and only Savior, Jesus Christ. This means that I have come to see the full mission as the joyful task of bringing others not only safely home to paradise, but also to the delightful "life in abundance" that Jesus promises here and now to all who follow him.

I was ordained in 1954. Twenty years later, Pope Paul VI convoked a Synod of Bishops on the theme of evangelization. This led to the writing of his dynamic encyclical, "On Evangelization in the Modern World" (*Evangelii Nuntiandi*). In that almost perfect teaching on the subject, this saintly and gentle pope states flat out and in no uncertain terms that the Church *exists* to evangelize. That alone should have awakened me, but it took a second pope to help fill out the picture in my own slower moving mind.

In this book, I will be sharing some of my thoughts and experiences with you. And I will enjoy doing so because that same old yearning experienced on the seminary roof a half-century ago seems to be acting up again!

Fr. Tom Forrest C.Ss.R.

Chapter 1

An Evangelizing and Nomadic Pope

I would like to express my thoughts about evangelization in the concrete context of a moment and a man. The moment is right now, as we are moving together into a new millennium of Christian history. The man is that exceptional spiritual guide whom the Holy Spirit placed on the throne of St. Peter so that the Church could have a sharp and clear vision for facing the challenges and utilizing the opportunities of the next thousand years. He is a man who has won the admiration and appreciation of millions, and his name is Pope John Paul II.

In writing about the pope, I have to begin by admitting right from the start that he is a man whom I love. His mission from God relates to all of us, but before spelling out that mission and how it impacts our lives and our moment of history, I would first like to talk about the man himself, pointing out some of the outstanding qualities I was able to observe and learn from on a personal level.

A Man of Love

First of all, I want to say that Pope John Paul II is a man of love. Early in the pope's pontificate, I was in the Piazza of St. Peter's during a Wednesday general audience that attracted some sixty thousand people. After the audience, His Holiness remained at the center of the piazza, praying and showing care for the sick and disabled until there were no more than a few thousand people huddled around him. By this time, even the Swiss Guards were a bit lax in their discipline, now leaning on their staffs rather than standing at full attention.

I spoke with Pope John Paul II for the first time in 1979, during a dialogue arranged by Cardinal Leon Joseph Suenens of Belgium. That first meeting lasted over an hour and a half, and saintly Bishop Uribe Jaramillo from Colombia was one of the participants. The bishop came out of the meeting looking at us in astonishment and saying with bewilderment, "My goodness, even my mother only kissed me on one cheek. The pope just kissed me twice." Kevin Ranaghan, a theologian from South Bend, Indiana, built like a lineman of the Notre Dame football team, exclaimed, "What a hug! He has arms of steel." Kevin was talking about a pope who was tiny in size compared with him, but immense in his ability to show affection for others.

At that time I had a Puerto Rican secretary by the name of Marta Vargas. Before this first dialogue, I was able to introduce her and other members of our office staff to His Holiness. During the dialogue, though, she and the rest of the staff had to wait in a room on the other side of a hall. When the dialogue ended and the pope was leaving, a formidable Swiss Guard stood outside the door to that room across the hall, making certain with outstretched arms that no one dashed forward to interfere with the passage of the Holy Father.

That was just fine with tiny Marta Vargas, who fit just right under the huge arm of the Swiss Guard. She stood there peeping underneath as the pope was leaving the meeting room. When he saw her, His Holiness gave a signal indicating that it was all right for her to approach. As he waved

His Holiness refused to leave until he had touched, blessed, and consoled every single sick person in the building. his hands in a signal to come forward, her legs began to wobble, but on a run she came. The pope asked her a few questions about herself and her family back home. Then he took her head in his hands and bent it forward to give her a kiss on the head—which I found out later was the traditional kiss of a Polish father.

I doubt that Marta washed her hair for the next two weeks. She kept walking around our office in a daze, mumbling every now and then those same words of amazement: "Who will ever believe that the pope kissed me on the top of my head?"

On one of my yearly trips to Calcutta, the Missionaries of Charity took me to visit Mother Teresa's famous home for the dying. On that visit, I prayed over a number of the sick and blessed the bodies of those who had recently passed away. Then the sisters told me about the Holy Father's visit to that same center of love only a few months earlier. Despite all the other events on his program for that busy day, His Holiness refused to leave until he had touched, blessed, and consoled every single sick person in the building. I had not done nearly that much, for the obvious reason that I simply do not compare with Pope John Paul II as a man of love.

The kindness and caring of Pope John Paul II are also evident in the way he listens to people. Once, when I was invited for dinner at the papal apartments in order to discuss the possibility of a decade of evangelization anticipating the Jubilee Year, the pope's words to me were, "Tell me about the letter you sent." Hearing the words, I became embarrassed, hesitant to begin a monologue while speaking with the pope himself. "But Holy Father," I said, "in answering I may have to speak for five or ten minutes." His answer was, "Five, ten, twenty! Talk!" That's the way the pope is in conversations. He wants to know everything he can about what is happening in the world and how it can best be served, and he is more ready to listen than anyone I have ever met.

While writing his magnificent biography of the pope, *Witness to Hope*, George Weigel said he was always open to new ideas and in possession of a seemingly limitless capacity to listen. On one occasion, he had to remind the pope, "But Holy Father, I'm the one who is here to ask the questions." The last time I had breakfast with the pope, an Irish and a Spanish priest were with me. When we came into the Piazza of St. Peter's after the breakfast, the Spanish priest lifted his arms in amazement and said, "I would never have believed that we could sit at a table like that and talk the way we just did with the pope himself." Pope John Paul is so ready and anxious to hear from others about what they are thinking and experiencing because he cares about and loves everyone in the world so much.

A Man of Prayer

My own personal experience of the prayer life of Pope John Paul II comes from the privilege of concelebrating at his private morning Masses on several occasions. Going to the little sacristy of the papal apartments, I had to pass the chapel door. Looking in as I passed, I could see His Holiness all in white, kneeling with bowed head at his *prie-dieu*. His way of celebrating the morning Eucharist couldn't have been more inspiring. I remember a young French woman commenting after one of these Masses, "I never fully appreciated the Eucharist until I saw how the pope says his Mass."

On our way to the papal library after the conclusion of the Mass, I again passed the chapel door, and the pope was there a second time, kneeling in prayer. After greeting His Holiness in the library, I was invited to the dining room for a short breakfast conversation. Passing the chapel door a third time, I saw the pope once again kneeling in prayer. After the breakfast, the Holy Father was the first to leave the dining room, and as I once more passed the chapel door, His Holiness was there a fourth time, absorbed in prayer. I read later that he customarily spends sixty to ninety minutes in prayer even before his early morning Mass. Sometimes he spends the entire night prostrate in prayer on the marble floor of that beautiful chapel.

In December 1994, when *Time* magazine declared him "Man of the Year," the publication described him as "an intellectual pope and a warrior pope. But he is also, and increasingly, a praying pope, a man rarely off his

MAN OF THE YEAR

POPE
JOHN PAUL II

knees." *Time* went on to write, "John Paul II is also a man for the rosary . . . he appears to say it continuously, and when not actually talking, his lips move all the time in silent, repetitive prayer."

Many of us quickly skip our own prayers with the excuse that we were just too busy to get them in. Without any doubt, the pope has far more to do than any of us, and yet it is estimated that he dedicates up to six hours each day in calm and peaceful prayer.

A Man of Work

I can easily understand how someone might say they would not mind having the honors, experience, and travels involved in being the pope. That's understandable, but if someone said to me that they would like to have the job of being the pope, they either know nothing about the job or they are in need of a good psychiatrist! From the little I have seen of his job, I wouldn't want it even for a single day. It is hard to imagine what it is like waking up in the morning with the thought, "Here I go again, with all those talks to give and listen to, all those meetings to attend and decisions to make, all those reports to study, and problems and tragedies to deal with."

I remember once meeting His Holiness at his summer house in Castel Gandolfo. After the meeting and Mass, I

If someone asked me for a single word to describe the role of a pope, the word I would choose is *martyrdom*.

was awaiting a bus to take me back into the city of Rome. Just then Arturo Mari, the official papal photographer, drove out of the papal palace and, seeing us, stopped to offer a lift into the city. Driving along with the man who accompanies the pope everywhere he travels, I did not hesitate to question him about this extraordinary man of God. "Does he ever take a vacation?" I asked. The photographer gave me a quick sideways glance that seemed to say, "You may be the one in need of the psychiatrist." "Vacation?" he responded. "I have been with this man for five years now, and in five years I haven't had a single day's vacation."

In the early days of Pope John Paul II's pontificate, I ran into the Spanish editor of the official Vatican newspaper, *L'Osservatore Romano*, and invited him for a cappuccino. As we sat talking, he said to me, "My goodness, this new pope is about to return to his native Poland for the first time since his election, and he has already written forty-five talks to be given during this one trip. We can't even get the talks translated in time for publication." Typically, Pope John Paul has not only given large numbers of instructions and exhortations on each of his more than ninety-eight pastoral trips, but also does his best to learn as much as he can of the language of each country he visits. I lived for several years with the young priest who tutored His Holiness in Portuguese prior to his first trip to Brazil.

An indication of how hard this man has worked over the years is the fact that he invites people to sit with him for discussions at breakfast, lunch, and dinner, something I believe no pope before him had ever done. This means that during all three of his meals, he is still hard at work, asking his questions and learning everything he can about the needs and situation of the Church and the world in search of new ways to understand and to serve.

A Man of Suffering

If someone asked me for a single word to describe the role of a pope, the word I would choose is *martyrdom*. I remember years ago reading a police story called *The New Centurions* that was made into a better-than-average film. In that story, a policeman was summoned to an apartment house to intervene in a violent domestic squabble. He headed up the staircase in the direction of all the shouting and noise, when the door to the couple's apartment suddenly opened, and out came the enraged husband, who planted himself at the top of the stairs and put a bullet through the stomach of the officer. The policeman survived the assault, but described the excruciating and unforgettable pain of having a bullet go through his stomach and the subsequent

Pope John Paul II visits his would-be assassin in prison to offer forgiveness.

terror at the thought of ever having it happen to him again. Pope John Paul II suffered that same experience when a Turkish would-be assassin sent a bullet into his stomach in the Piazza of St. Peter's.

No matter how great the physical pain of that attack, far greater was the emotional pain the pontiff suffered when a schismatic priest attempted to stab him to death in front of the Shrine of Our Lady of Fatima in Portugal. I don't doubt for a moment that attacks from within the Church cause him more anguish than even the worst attacks coming from outside the Church. Once when I heard a young priest in a far eastern country vehemently attacking the pope, I couldn't resist asking him, "Do you really know anything about what it's like to be the pope?"

People today often comment that "he looks so tired and worn out." That is true, and there are good reasons for being physically and emotionally weary. That never stops him, though, and he remains as courageous as he is hard working. If someone says to me, "Don't go down that street; there is danger and violence at the end of the block," I thank them and go down another street. John Paul II does the opposite. You say something like that to him, and he answers, "That's where I am needed," and down that street he goes!

Several months after a serious operation, he headed for Sudan. No one goes to Sudan for a vacation or just to view the beautiful sights. It is a land of famine, religious persecution, and constant civil war, and that's why the pope went there. He was abused on his trip to Nicaragua during the reign of the Sandinistas in 1983, and it was hard to keep him from going to Lebanon during its most difficult moments of civil war. Despite all the difficulties and dangers and his failing physical health, this pope kept planning future pastoral travels to wherever he was needed and could do some good.

Bishop John Magee, the Irish secretary of three popes and a former missionary in Africa, told a story that impressed me with the Holy Father's courage for confronting dangers and difficulties. Bishop Magee was first the secretary of Pope Paul VI, and then secretary of both John Paul I and John Paul II. In a dinner that we had together, he related how Pope John Paul I had felt uneasy in his first month on the job, apprehensive about facing the challenges and responsibilities of the papacy. Thirty-three days after his election, the saintly and fatherly John Paul I was taken to heaven.

Now the new Pope John Paul II is eating lunch with Monsignor Magee and a group of bishops and priests from the pope's former archdiocese of Krakow, Poland. One of the close friends of His Holiness asked what you or I might possibly ask a friend of ours who, to our amazement, had just become the Pope of Rome: "What does it feel like," the friend asked, "to wake up in the morning and remember 'I'm the pope'?" John Paul II thought for only a moment or two and then without hesitation responded, "Well, from the moment that I said '*Accepto*' [the traditional Latin word for accepting the election], I've felt like I've always been the pope!" God chose Karol Wojtyla for the job, and God gave him all of the courage and strength needed for facing the dangers, difficulties, and unavoidable pain.

A Man of Many Charisms

Without any doubt, this pope is a man of the Holy Spirit. He is the world's number one charismatic—not in the sense of belonging to a particular movement in the Church, but in the truer sense of being exceptionally gifted and empowered by the Holy Spirit. He makes constant references to the Holy Spirit in his encyclicals and apostolic letters and in all of the talks he gives around the world. He has written a specific encyclical totally dedicated to the indispensable role of the Holy Spirit in the fulfillment of the Church's mission and the attainment of our individual holiness.

In that first meeting back in 1979, we reported to the Holy Father our personal experiences of the New Pentecost that were spreading like wildfire across the world. At the end of this report and after a short film that was shown to the pope, His Holiness stood up and said to us: "Now let me tell you about my own charismatic way. When I was a young schoolboy, I was having trouble with mathematics. So my wise father sat me down and made me the gift of a little prayer book. He opened the book to the prayer, 'Come Holy Spirit.' Then he said to me, 'Now, son, I want you to make me a promise. Never begin a day of your life without beginning that day by saying this prayer.' "

After recounting this story of his early childhood, the man who was now Bishop of Rome added with almost childlike simplicity, "For over fifty years now, I have been an obedient son to my father." With those simple words, he revealed to us the secret of what has made him the most personally powerful and influential man of our times. His secret to power is the fact that he begins each day of his life by begging inspiration, wisdom, patience, and holiness from the Third Person of the Blessed Trinity, the divinely promised source of it all.

The pope is so rich in the gifts of the Holy Spirit that a whole book could be written solely on that topic. However, for our purposes, I will share only about his charism for youth and his contagious hope and joy.

First of all, he has an amazing and almost inexplicable gift for enthusing and inspiring young people. He calls these youths the *hope*, the *future*, and the *tomorrow* of the Church. I had a small role in planning teachings for the very first World Youth Day, which took place in Rome at the beginning of Holy Week in 1984. At first it was estimated that one hundred thousand young people would attend, but that estimate soon dropped to only forty

thousand. The actual number that participated was 250,000, and even some very dry theologians admitted that those young people "changed the city of Rome."

The concluding Mass took place on Palm Sunday. As the Holy Father processed through the piazza, that quarter of a million young people went wild with English shouts of "John Paul II, we love you," and echoing cries in Spanish of *"Juan Pablo Segundo, te quiere todo el mundo!"* As he walked through St. Peter's Piazza, the pope carried in one arm a large branch of palm, and with his free hand he held his famous crosier crucifix. Hoping to catch a glance their way, the young people roared as he passed, "Holy Father, Holy Father!" Walking along with arms occupied by crosier and palm branch, the best the pope could do in response to their enthusiasm was to wave back with a wiggle of the pinky finger on the hand that held the crosier. That tiny wiggle of recognition was all it took to win their love.

As the Holy Father processed through the piazza, a quarter of a million young people went wild with English shouts of "John Paul II, we love you!"

After the Eucharistic celebration was over, the crowd of other tourists that had spilled from the piazza to the Tiber River melted away, but the young people were still in the piazza dancing and shouting. Suddenly that famous window in the Apostolic Palace opened up, and the Man in White appeared on the balcony. He held a microphone and called down to the dancing youths, "Go home. You've been here all morning and must be hungry," referring to the fact that the service had lasted almost four hours. Then the pope himself began to chant in his deep bass voice, "John Paul II, he loves you! John Paul II, he loves you!" That little expression of affection sent the crowd dancing even more wildly.

On another occasion, I visited the pope with a group of four hundred youths from the Italian movement, *Communione e Liberazione*. The occasion was the Holy Father's name-day feast of St. Charles, and the place was the courtyard of St. Damasus, just below the papal apartments. The Holy Father stood this time on a small balcony only one or two steps above the ground. Two young women came forward with a large and beautifully decorated cake. The pope invited them to come around and step out on the balcony with him. Then he asked them to cut him a slice of the cake. When they did so, he surprised them by saying, "Thank you very much, and now have a bite." Thus they, not he, were the first to sample their very tasty gift.

Many have commented that this pope is always animated and overjoyed by the young people crowding around him. The truth is that he has a magical ability to animate and excite them. Prior to World Youth Day in Paris, one French newspaper wrote: "Young people of France aren't interested in that old man. They are predicting that five hundred thousand will come to see him, but the crowd won't be any larger than fifty thousand." The actual number who showed up was 1.1 million, and in Rome for the World Youth Day during the Jubilee Year, the number grew to two million. He undoubtedly attracts these multitudes of young people because he authentically loves them, considers them extraordinarily valuable, treats them with genuine warmth and affection, spends time with them, and shows them a delightful sense of humor.

Pope John Paul II also bubbles with charisms of hope and joy. On a number of occasions, I visited countries such as Ghana, Canada, Spain, Puerto Rico, Poland, Ireland, Colombia, and France very soon after a papal visit. It was easy to observe that Pope John Paul II always leaves behind a trail of excitement and joy. There are thousands of photographs of throngs meeting and reaching out to the Holy Father, and all those faces in the crowds are glowing with twinkling eyes and broad smiles.

When in Spain after one of those papal visits, I read a magazine that summed up the visit with these words, "The most extraordinary thing about John Paul II is his vigorous hope." He wrote a bestselling book entitled *Crossing the Threshold of Hope*, and George Weigel entitled his biography *Witness to Hope*. The Pope daringly prophesies a "*new springtime* for the Church and the world," and in one conversation I heard him predict that a new faith would be returning to western Europe from—of all places—Russia, the very nation that for fifty years held his native and beloved Poland in bondage. It is easy to see that Pope John Paul II is truly a man of hope and joy, and one of his very obvious missions is to shout out that message of hope and spread that joy around the whole world.

The Definition of His Pontificate

Until now, I have been speaking in only a general way about the personality and qualities of this impressive and inspiring man of God. All of this was only a preparation for what I now want to say about his mission and his moment in history.

Numerous books, talks, tapes, films, and countless articles have been produced describing the character and explaining the mission of Pope John Paul II. They are all very interesting, but we don't really need any of them to understand his pontificate. Pope John Paul himself tells us in so many words exactly why he is the pope and what is the purpose of his pontificate. He did this in Mexico City on May 6, 1990, and as we read his words, it is important to observe the language of discernment that he uses. He is not telling us what he is planning or what he would like to accomplish, but rather what God has planned and willed in placing him on the throne of Peter. "The Lord, the master of history and of our destinies, has wished that my pontificate be that of a pilgrim pope of evangelization, walking down the roads of the world, bringing to all peoples the message of salvation."

These words are what lead me to see Pope John Paul II as a *nomadic* and *kerygmatic* pope.

A nomad is a tent-dweller, always on the go. "A Pilgrim walking down the roads of the world" is the way the pope describes himself, and by latest count as I write this, he has made more than ninety-eight pastoral trips to over 130 countries to establish his claim to the title, while also making constant weekend trips to the many parishes of his own episcopal diocese of Rome. In the city of Rome, he is definitely a Peter, but by traveling the world, he is also a Paul, allowing neither sickness nor weariness to slow him down.

Kerygma is the Greek word for the charism and mission of proclaiming the Good News of Jesus Christ to those people who have never had an opportunity to hear it. When John Paul II calls himself "a pope of evangelization bringing the message of salvation to all peoples," he is telling us that the mission God has given him is definitely kerygmatic.

On October 16, 1978, white smoke floated out over the Basilica of St. Peter and crowds quickly gathered in the piazza to hear the name of the successor to John Paul I. Five days after his election, and during the homily of his inauguration as the new pontiff, the Holy Father spoke these historic words: "Do not be afraid. Throw open the doors to Christ!" In that dynamic way, he told the whole world that he recognized fear to be our most basic problem, and that the most effective answer to that problem was Christ the Redeemer!

Five years later, the pope was in Haiti, poorest nation of the Americas, where he made a dynamic call for an evangelization that needed to be "new in fervor, expression, and method." From that day on, in every nation he visited and to the great throngs coming to hear him, he never missed an opportunity to repeat his call for a new evangelization. This traveling and evangelizing pope was consistent in proclaiming Jesus Christ as our only Savior, and in challenging every member of the Catholic Church to join with him in carrying the Good News of salvation to the ends of the earth.

He is an evangelizer, totally focused on the most fundamental of all truths: the fact that the Messiah promised to Adam, Abraham, Moses, David, Isaiah, and all mankind has come, and his name is Jesus of Nazareth! This nomadic and kerygmatic pope is very clearly energized and impelled by the truth that "there is no other name under heaven given among mortals by which we must be saved" (Acts 4:12). On his second papal visit to the United States, he was greeted at the Miami airport by then-President Ronald Reagan. He began the visit stating clearly that he had come "to proclaim the Gospel of Jesus Christ to those who freely choose to listen, to tell again the story of God's love for the world" (September 10, 1987). From there to every continent he traveled, he carried and cried out the same Good News.

But to those two words, *nomadic* and *kerygmatic*, I want to add a third. Pope John Paul II is also *dynamic*. That added adjective comes from the Greek word meaning power, and during the past two decades, John Paul II has

John Paul II has definitely been a man with a power for making things happen.

definitely been a man with a power for making things happen, and happen they did!

The Weigel biography describes him as a man who "never had a bank account, never wrote a check, never had any personal money." He often slept on the floor, and possessions meant so little to him that (except for his skis and hiking equipment), he could have been mistaken for a beggar (*Witness to Hope*, p. 119). These facts make us curious to know where his immense earth-moving power comes from, and Weigel attributes his great pastoral success to his priestly holiness and commitment to the care of souls (p. 193). Some may doubt that holiness and commitment alone can produce enough dynamism in a person to lead *Time* magazine to place him on its cover as "Man of the Year," but the facts are there.

Vittorio Messori, editor of the Holy Father's bestselling book, *Crossing the Threshold of Hope*, goes into detail describing the holiness and commitment that generate this dynamism. "This is a pope who is impatient in his apostolic zeal; a shepherd to whom the usual paths always seem insufficient; who looks to every means to spread the Good News to men: who—evangelically—wants to shout from the rooftops . . . that there is hope" (p. VIII). Weigel himself is even more descriptive in portraying this dynamic and very modern pope:

"He ... redefines the Catholic Church's relationship to Judaism ... preaches to Muslim teenagers in a packed stadium in Casablanca, and describes marital intimacy as an icon of the triune God. After ... the world media pronounces him a dying, if heroic, has-been, ... he publishes an international bestseller translated into forty languages, gathers the largest crowds in human history ... Addressing the United Nations in 1995, he defends the universality of human rights. ... Two days later, the irrepressible pontiff does a credible imitation of Jack Benny during Mass in Central Park, and the cynical New York press loves it." (*Witness to Hope*, pp. 3 and 4)

For several years now, I have ended talks on evangelization by mentioning John Wayne, Hollywood's most famous cowboy. In scores of films, Wayne used the same words to signal that the time has come for dynamic action: taking off his big and dusty cowboy hat, looking around a final time, waving the hat above his head, and shouting out, "Okay men, move it out!" I then ask how many in the audience ever saw a John Wayne movie. Even in a meeting of animated young people in Muslim Malaysia, almost every hand went up. My next question is, "And when John Wayne yelled out those words, how many of his men moved?" The answer comes back loud and clear: "All of them!" My final question is, "And how many of his battles did John Wayne win?" The answer a second time is: "All of them!"

© Bettmann/Corbis

JOHN WAYNE (J).

Catholics really don't need a fictional movie hero. The Church offers someone better, and his name is John Paul II!

They may have forgotten that one lost battle, the Alamo. Even so, the example is clear, though Catholics really don't need a fictional movie hero. The Church offers someone better, and his name is John Paul II! From the moment he became pope, John Paul II has been calling the Catholic Church to forceful and decisive action! In his encyclical, *Redemptoris Missio* (On the Mission of the Redeemer), and repeatedly in subsequent apostolic letters, he sends out a thrilling vision that only the spiritually deaf could fail to hear. If in so many movies, John Wayne took that final discerning look around before shouting out his call for action, this great pope of our times does exactly the same, and he is not playing a part in a fantasy. He is telling us not only that the moment is right, but also that victory is near:

> God is opening before the Church the horizons of a humanity more fully prepared for the sowing of the Gospel. I sense that the moment has come to

commit all of the Church's energies to a new evangelization.

Today, as never before, the Church has the opportunity of bringing the Gospel . . . to all people and
nations. I see the dawning of a new missionary age,
which will become a radiant day bearing an abundant
harvest, if all Christians . . . respond with generosity
and holiness to the calls and challenges of our time.

(*Redemptoris Missio*, 3, 92)

John Wayne pranced around on his big horse, waving
an oversized hat to animate people to heroic deeds. No
cowboy hero in the movies has ever sent out a more challenging call than Pope John Paul II. The Catholic Church
today has a dynamic leader, and he is shouting out a
dynamic call to action. Victory will be ours if we too make
the discernment that the time is right and dynamically
"MOVE IT OUT!" Our only timely response is dynamic
action supporting a dynamic pope.

Let's take a careful look at the action he is calling us
to: the delightful and salvific task of continuing the mission of Christ that we call *evangelization*. ∏

Chapter 2

Evangelization
Is Everyone's Job

Forty is a very biblical number, perhaps even mystical. The number appears at least 145 times throughout the Bible. We read that in the time of Noah, a rain lasting forty days and forty nights brought on the great flood (Genesis 7:4). God poured down manna upon the wandering Israelites as Moses led them through the desert for forty years (Exodus 16:35). On the strength of bread and water supplied by an angel, Elijah traveled forty days and forty nights before reaching Horeb, the Holy Mountain of God (1 Kings 19:8). Jesus prepared for his public life by fasting and praying in the desert for forty days and forty nights (Matthew 4:2). After rising from the dead in proof of his divinity, Jesus remained on earth, revealing himself to his disciples and preparing them for the mission that would send them to the ends of the earth, for another forty days prior to his ascension (Acts 1:3).

The number forty also seems to relate clearly to our present moment in Church history. From 1960, when Pope John XXIII was sending out his call for a Second Vatican Council, until the wonderfully successful Jubilee Year 2000, we have been experiencing forty years of church renewal, envisioned by Pope John as an opportunity for opening church windows and allowing a fresh new breeze to blow through our dusty and ancient halls.

What are we implying when we say that the Church is in need of renewal? In the spirit of Pope John Paul II, who has been humbly begging forgiveness around the world for certain errors and failures of the Church, we too can confess that something is lacking in our modern era of Church history. Some things that should be done have been left undone, or at best not done nearly well enough.

If you ask a number of bishops, priests, and qualified experts, you will no doubt accumulate a variety of answers to the questions, "Exactly what is wrong with the Church? What is being left undone? What is not being accomplished with satisfactory vitality and success?" My own way of explaining why the Church of our times is in need of renewal is by pointing out that over the centuries the People of God have grown *passive*, becoming, as Cardinal Leon Joseph Suenens of Belgium liked to say, "more *frozen* than *chosen*." They have become sleepy, going to church once a week only to sit for an hour on a very hard wooden bench.

Sleepiness, though, has nothing to do with the job of being a Christian. Christianity is a life to be lived, and lived to the hilt! It is a job to be accomplished at any cost, a mission whose fulfillment determines the ultimate success of our lives. Jesus tells us in no uncertain terms that we must bear fruit in abundance, "fruit that will last" (John 15:2,16). Any branch that remains barren will be pruned away and cast into the fire (15:6).

Who gets the blame if so many—and perhaps even most—Catholics have come to believe that they are accomplishing their whole job simply by making a Sunday trip to church to attend a service that hopefully will never last longer than an hour? I don't think the blame goes to those in the benches, but rather to the priests in the pulpit. Not deliberately perhaps, but over the centuries and

Earlier days with young friends from Guatamala.

the years, they allowed the development of a monopoly that assigned all of the ministries of the Church, together with all the pastoral gifts of the Holy Spirit, as an exclusive right of the clergy.

When giving talks, I often make an admittedly exaggerated joke here by saying that until Pope John XXIII came along with his prophetic vision for a Second Vatican Council, the laity in the Church were offered only three jobs, and women got none of them. In ascending order of importance, the three jobs were: Altar boys can bring up the wine and water at Mass; ushers can take up the collection; and those with voices of authority can call out the numbers at Bingo! Beyond that, the priest did just about everything, which means that a great deal was left undone. How could only four hundred thousand priests in a world of more than one billion Catholics adequately shepherd all of the sheep all by themselves, and manage to do an excellent job?

Once when giving a retreat to priests in Guatemala, I asked how many sheep they felt able to adequately shepherd, in fulfillment of the biblical ideals of good shepherding found in Ezekiel 34, Psalm 23, and John 10. In these texts, and in response to the example Jesus the Good Shepherd gives us, they must protect, feed, heal, instruct, lead, and love the sheep to the point of dying for them. The priests answered, "Maybe thirty!" To this I responded, "Perhaps no more than fifteen."

A priest in Central America told me that he was the only shepherd for a parish of 120,000. On the day that a newly ordained priest in Venezuela was leaving the seminary, he was given a parish without a church and rectory, but with a Catholic population of 88,000. The largest parish I ever visited encircles half a million Catholics served by twelve priests, but I know of an area in Africa with a population of 750,000 and only a single priest. For six years, I worked in a parish of the Dominican Republic with fifty thousand souls scattered through some of the highest and most isolated mountains of the Caribbean. How could we ever believe that priests alone can respond successfully to that much responsibility?

As this idea of a clerical monopoly took hold, even the vocabulary of the People of God grew passive. People could be heard saying that they were going to church only to *hear* Mass, and some did exactly that, making it hard to get them even to answer "Amen" and enthusiastically sing a hymn. They *listened* to the sermon and *received* the sacraments, but we are called to do far more than simply *listen* and *receive*.

How passively and negatively we talk about doing the utterly delightful and satisfying will of God the Father.

How about putting into practice with fierce determination the reality communicated with every word and gesture of the commissioning sacraments being conferred? Baptism, for example, makes us nothing less than adopted children of God, chosen princes and princesses in the Father's kingdom. This means that from that instant on, we are expected to live every moment of our lives in a way that honors our royal heritage and brings joy to the heart of our heavenly Father.

As attitudes of passivity grew, even some very pious-sounding phrases that entered the Catholic vocabulary became so passive that they were actually offensive and insulting to God. How about this as an example: "I am going to *resign* myself to the will of God." In Psalm 40:9 we read the words, "To do your will is my *delight*" (NAB; italics added.). If someone invited me to a wonderful dinner at the best restaurant in town or for a few weeks' vacation on a sunny Caribbean island in the middle of frigid February, would my best and only response be to put on a long face and simply "*resign* myself"? Yet, that's how passively and negatively we talk about doing the utterly delightful and satisfying will of God the Father.

Eventually the laity found themselves with only one real activity regarding the Church, and that was to criticize!

While standing or sitting perfectly still themselves, they could point a finger and calmly ask why the bishop and the priests weren't doing more, why the sisters and religious today couldn't do any better, or why, in the midst of so much suffering and injustice, the priests and the Church were failing to serve human needs more dynamically and effectively.

A People with a Mission

The hard fact is that whenever any of us begins to criticize the Church (and there is need for constructive and *loyal* criticism), we must first remember that WE are the Church. The mission of the Church belongs to each and every one of us, and this means that we must begin our criticism by taking an honest look at ourselves, to see if we are doing—and doing well—the job God Almighty gave us as baptized members of his Church.

In taking that look, we should begin with an evaluation of how well we are doing the job of sharing Christ with others, the inescapable Christian duty we call *evangelization*. I remember once asking Mother Teresa how she would define evangelization. She thought for a moment, and then answered with a clarity and insight that surpassed that of most theologians: "To evangelize means that you have Jesus in your own heart, and then you carry him to the hearts of others."

Jesus was explicit in telling us that he was sent by the Father and anointed by the Holy Spirit to announce good news (Luke 4:18,43). He also tells us that, "As the Father has sent me, so I send you" (John 20:21). This realization

that Jesus has made us responsible for proclaiming him as good news comes as a big surprise to most Catholics. They mistakenly think that it is the task only of priests or nuns and foreign missionaries, but that is not true! Evangelization is the mission of all Christians.

Back in 1988, I was in the town of Trujillo, north of Lima, Peru, where twenty-five thousand people gathered to initiate a decade of evangelization in preparation for the Year 2000. A large stage was erected in the middle of the town square, and stretching across the stage was a great banner trumpeting the words, "It is not enough that you know Jesus. You must make him known to others!"

I've quoted those words all over the world, because they echo what the Church has been telling us again and again during these forty years of renewal. The Vatican II document,

"On the Missionary Activity of the Church," declares that, "The whole Church is missionary, and the work of evangelization is a basic duty of the People of God" (*Ad Gentes*, 35). As a consequence of an episcopal synod on the theme of evangelization, Pope Paul VI wrote a startlingly beautiful apostolic letter entitled, "On Evangelization in the Modern World." In it he succinctly and forcefully stated that "evangelizing is . . . the grace and vocation proper to the Church, her deepest identity. The Church exists in order to evangelize" (*Evangelii Nuntiandi*, 14). This crystal-clear statement can make us ask how important is the Church's existence if she is failing to evangelize, since that is the God-given purpose of her existence.

Pope John Paul II is even more decisive in his document, "On the Mission of the Redeemer." He tells us first of all that, "No believer in Christ, no institution of the Church can avoid this supreme duty: to proclaim Christ to all peoples," and later adds these words of emphasis: "Since they are members of the Church by virtue of their baptism, all Christians share responsibility for missionary activity" (*Redemptoris Missio*, 3, 77). The Good News is simply too good to be left as the message and mission of those few Christians who fall into the category of clergy and religious.

Jesus is the best gift any of us has to share. It is certainly a kindness to take someone out for a lovely meal in a good restaurant, but Scripture doesn't proclaim, "Blessed are those who eat well." What we read is, "Blessed are they who hear the word of God" (Luke 11:28). Those who feast in an excellent restaurant again grow hungry quickly enough. Those who come to know and love and follow Jesus Christ are offered an eternal freedom from all hunger and thirst.

A Religion of Love

Of all the religions of the world, Christianity is the easiest to define. The religions of ancient Greece and Rome, with their multitude of gods and all the wars and jealousies that divide them, are not easy to map out or explain. Not any easier are the faiths of the Hindus or Buddhists. Easier perhaps is the Muslim religion with its concept of Allah, the one true God. But clearest and easiest of all is Christianity, a faith that can be defined and explained with one tiny four-letter word, and that word is L O V E.

As Christians we adore the one true God, whom St. John tells us "is love" (1 John 4:8). We have a Savior who is that divine love made visible so that we can learn from him how to love. He tells us that love of God is the first and greatest commandment, and that second to it is love of neighbor. Our Lord's new commandment is that we love one another in exactly the same way he loves us, by dying for us on the cross. This makes love the measuring rod of our Christianity, meaning that we are authentic disciples of Jesus Christ only to the degree that we have learned from our Master and Model of Love how to live a life of love—how to live the life of God himself.

If love is the rule of thumb for measuring our Christianity, there are some hard questions relating to the task of evangelization that we need to ask:

■ If I know the Word that gives eternal life but speak that Word to no one in order that they too may have life, have I learned from Jesus how to love?

■ If I know the only Name given to man by which he is to be saved but offer salvation to no one by revealing that name, or if I possess the truth that sets us free but with it make no effort to set even a single prisoner free, have I learned Christ's lesson of love?

■ If I walk in the Light of Life but with that light illuminate the pathway of not a single other person, and if I feast on the bread that ends all hunger and the drink that takes away all thirst but lead no one to the Eucharistic banquet table, where is the love of Christ in me?

■ If in Jesus Christ I made contact with the Wisdom from above so that I now enjoy life in abundance, but I share that wisdom and joy with not one single person, have I learned the lesson that Christ came from heaven to teach me?

■ In other words, am I a real Christian if I do nothing and make no effort to bring Christ as Good News to those who might otherwise never come to know him?

Here is another little list, this time of the names and titles Christ willingly and joyfully assigns to us:

■ He makes all of us *coworkers* (1 Corinthians 3:9) with him in the vineyard of the Lord, and that means we had better get to work.

■ He calls us the *salt of the earth* (Matthew 5:13), so if the world is losing its flavor, who has the blame?

■ He refers to us as the *light of the world* (Matthew 5:14), so who is responsible for all the blindness if millions and literally billions still walk in darkness?

■ He calls us to be *fishers of men and women* (Matthew 4:19), *shepherds* sent in quest of his lost sheep (Matthew 10:6).

■ He sends us forth as his *witnesses* to the very ends of the earth (Acts 1:8), commissioned like John the Baptist to cry out in the wilderness, "Make straight the way of the Lord" (John 1:23).

This job is more important than showing people how to become millionaires, more important than discovering a cure for cancer or AIDS, and even more important than feeding the hungry children of Africa. The fact is that only by teaching the love of Christ in ways that lead others to share their time and possessions with the sick, the hungry, and the suffering will we eventually succeed in feeding all those hungry babies and finding an answer for all that suffering.

Shout It from the Housetops

Despite the overwhelming importance of leading millions to understand and live the love of Jesus Christ, it is not that easy to find great numbers of active, joyful, and dedicated evangelizers. Some Catholics complain that even from our Sunday pulpits, the Good News sounds more like a funeral dirge or works more like a cozy pillow lulling us to sleep than like the sword of truth and war boots that carry us into the joyful battle of overcoming selfishness with love (Ephesians 5:14; 6:15,17). A few "scholars" are even making God's Word of Life, Christ's life-giving message of love, ring out more like the "great maybe" than like the heavenly revealed truth by which we can safely live and for which we should be confidently ready to die.

We can safely leave this universal call to evangelize in the hands of others, if we remain certain that every nation and all mankind will hear the Good News and come to love and follow Jesus to paradise even if we mentioned his beautiful name to absolutely no one. But if, in Divine Providence, there is but one person in my family, at the office or factory where I work, in the school or college where I study, or in any of the places where I shop and recreate, who needs to hear the Good News from me or else will never hear it and know salvation, my failure to communicate that Good News could be my most serious sin of omission! Scripture warns about the severe punishment awaiting those who fail to offer a glass of water requested in the name of Jesus. Imagine what might be the punishment awaiting someone who lazily neglects to share that name itself with those thirsting for the peace and joy that only our Lord's name can bring (Matthew 25:35).

I don't think I would have the courage to warn about these punishments unless the popes themselves hadn't already given us the warnings. I usually paraphrase the words of Pope Paul VI, telling how he warns us that we may not be on the way to heaven ourselves if we are doing nothing to take others along with us. His actual words are these: "Can we gain salvation if through neglect or fear or shame—what St. Paul called 'blushing for the Gospel'— . . . we fail to preach it?" (*Evangelii Nuntiandi*, 80). As always, the phrasing of Pope John Paul II is even more forceful: "Those who are incorporated into the Catholic Church ought to sense . . . their greater obligation of *bearing witness to the faith*. . . . If they fail to respond to this grace in thought, word, and deed, not only will they not be saved, they will be judged more severely" (*Redemptoris Missio*, 11).

What a failure for the Church, if most Catholics have never heard that the Church exists to evangelize! What a danger for all members of the Church if they remain ignorant of an obligation that could help open for them the gates of paradise!

What do most of us do when we have heard very good news? Do we say, "We're Catholics, and Catholics don't

Joe won only one hundred million dollars, rated by St. Paul as nothing more than garbage compared to "the surpassing value of knowing Christ Jesus."

repeat Good News, so shush, keep quiet, don't say a word"? No! Whenever we have some really good news to tell, the usual thing is to excitedly want to be the first to share it. Let's imagine for example that we have a very nice elderly neighbor, who is now almost totally blind. Every now and then, we bring him some hot soup, come by to straighten up the yard, and do a bit of shopping for him. One day he says to us, "You know, my life has gotten pretty dull. Why don't you spark it up a bit by buying me a lottery ticket each week? I can't read, but when the winning number is announced in the newspaper, you could look it up for me and tell me if I've won." You do this for a whole year, and for a second and a third year. Then on a certain Wednesday, you pick up the paper to read the winning number and almost fall down in amazement. It's Joe's number staring back at you from the page. Your friend just won one hundred million dollars!

All right, you now have the good news, but Joe does-n't. So what do you do? Do you look out your upstairs window to see Joe puttering away in his garden next door and then yell down only to say, "Hi Joe, how are the roses?" I don't think so! I think you almost fall out the window with the excitement of being the first one to tell Joe the big news. With a loud whoop, you yell out delightedly, "Hey, Joe, you won!"

But Joe only won one hundred million dollars, rated by St. Paul as nothing more than garbage compared to "the surpassing value of knowing Christ Jesus" (Philippians 3:8). Through Jesus Christ we have won the pearl of greatest price, the hidden treasure more valuable than anything else—forgiveness of all our sins and eternal glory in heaven, where we will be living with God himself.

Let's use another example, this time from the world of sports.

Winning More Than a Tin Cup!

The most watched of all great sporting events is the World Soccer Cup, taking place in different major cities around the world every four years. In 1998, the Cup finals took place in Paris, and the two teams playing were Brazil and France. Brazil is a nation of nearly hysterical soccer fans, and it is easy to imagine the excitement of the French playing in their beautiful capital city of Paris.

At the end of that emotional game, there were only two kinds of athletes left on the playing field: the winners (the French) and the losers (the Brazilians). Between these two groups of prime athletes, there was a tremendous emotional difference. That renowned philosopher of modern times, the sports announcer, went first into the locker room of the Brazilians, thrusting his television camera into their faces, and asked that brilliant and meaningful question, "How do you feel?" The Brazilians couldn't answer. They were absolutely heartbroken, lost in the depths of despair, living the most painful moment of their entire lives, and wondering how they would ever have the courage to return home to the nation they failed. They had just lost the *Tin Cup!*

Then the sports announcer headed for the locker room of the French team, and it was a different story. They were jumping and shouting for joy, hugging and kissing each other cheek-to-cheek in the style of the French, bathing themselves in champagne, and searching for more ways to express their ecstatic joy at victory. In their entire lives, they had never lived a more delightful moment. They had just won the *Tin Cup!*

Living on this planet right now, there are more than six billion—six thousand million—human beings. Every single one of them will one day reach the end of their game, the all-important moment of death. At that moment there can be only two kinds of human beings, the winners or losers. There is no *third* way for any of us to end our life here on earth. At that deciding moment, we will not have won or lost only a *Tin Cup*, destined some day to rust away and turn to dust. The prize, lost or won, will be the eternal and unimaginable joys of paradise, the inexpressibly beautiful vision of the face of God.

Those who lost the World Soccer Cup in 1998 had a chance to win it in 2002. Those who won the Cup in 2002 risk losing it in the city of the next World Cup tournament. It's not that way at the end of the tournament of life. Those

What makes the far greater difference between winners and losers of eternal joy at the moment of death? The only answer is successful evangelization!

who lose the sight and joy of God do so forever, and those winning the victory will enjoy it forever. Dante wasn't just being poetic when he wrote over the gates of hell those serious and frightening words, "Abandon all hope, you who enter here."

In that world championship soccer game, exactly what brought about that immense difference between the deep despair of the losers and the ecstatic joy of the winners? We know the answer: a quick and accurate movement of the foot, adding a single and decisive point to the score. What makes the far greater difference between winners and losers of eternal joy at the moment of death? The only answer is successful evangelization!

Victors in the Game of Life

The ultimate value and success of every human life depends upon hearing, believing, and living the Good News of Jesus Christ. That's why Jesus instructed us to "go into all the world and proclaim the good news to the whole creation," explaining that "the one who believes and is baptized will be saved" (Mark 16:15-16). Using a more modern vocabulary, Jesus could have ended these words with the phrase "will be a winner." John the Apostle brings home this same truth, explaining that "the Father has sent his Son as the Savior of the world. God abides in those who confess that Jesus is the Son of God, and they abide in God" (1 John 4:14-15). With these words, John gives us his own description of the winning points in the all-important game of life: whatever enables us to acknowledge Christ as the only source of our sanctifying union with God.

If coming to know Christ as our only safe way home to the Father's house is the decisive factor determining the winners and losers in the game of life, how can we possibly doubt the importance of evangelization, our first duty as baptized Christians? Paul becomes extremely logical about this when writing to the Romans: "Everyone who calls on the name of the Lord shall be saved. But how are they to call on one in whom they have not believed? And how are they to believe in one of whom they have never heard? And how are they to hear without someone to proclaim him?" (Romans 10:13-14). These words tell us that our efforts to echo the words of eternal life can be the deciding factor between the agony of defeat and the ecstasy of victory at that decisive time of life: our moment of death.

With these clear and simple words, Christ commissioned all of us: "Preach as you go, saying, 'The kingdom of heaven is at hand'" (Matthew 10:7). As we travel our God-given pathways through life, every one of us must be a carrier of that delightful Good News that God's kingdom is here, and that the King of Glory is among us, loving and teaching us, leading and protecting us, healing and forgiving us, saving us from our sins, lighting our pathway home, and incorporating us safely into the kingdom of our heavenly Father.

My own pathway has already taken me to more than one hundred countries and I don't know how many cities and towns. On the many trips I've taken, I have met people who will never meet you or hear your voice. You, in your turn, have your own pathways, and as you travel them, you meet people who will never see me or hear my voice. For whatever pathway we travel, God gives us the same instructions: "Announce the Good News of the saving presence of Christ the King among us!" If all of us take this commission seriously, and commit ourselves to accomplishing our job, the Good News will be carried to the very ends of the earth. The whole world will change, heading once more toward the paradise of holiness and love that God, from the beginning, intended it to be.

I once had an opportunity of seeing exactly how dear and great Mother Teresa of Calcutta lived out this particular instruction. She was with us in the first Worldwide Retreat for Priests that I organized in Vatican City in 1984. An official of the Vatican came to me in the Papal Audience Hall, saying that the cardinals were awaiting Mother Teresa in the synod hall of bishops. When we entered the hall, it was crowded not only with cardinals, archbishops, and bishops, but also with papal diplomats from dozens of nations around the world.

"Preach as you go" are the words of our commission, and the synod hall of bishops was where Mother Teresa was

As we travel our God-given pathways through life, every one of us must be a carrier of that delightful Good News.

going on this particular morning. So, she followed the instructions of Jesus and made the announcement. I can remember the exact words she said to all of those very important people: "Love Jesus; believe in Jesus; listen to Jesus; pray to Jesus; follow Jesus; love Jesus." With those simple words, she confidently *evangelized* that impressive group of dignitaries for no other reason than that it was exactly what Jesus had instructed her to do. On that particular day, it just happened that she was given an exceptional opportunity for doing the job.

This mission of sharing Christ is so important that it cannot be left undone. We cannot be frightened by dangers or difficulties! We cannot be distracted! We cannot fail! Others may turn away with feelings of fear and insecurity, but not us. We have the answer! We know that "there is no other name . . . by which we must be saved" (Acts 4:12). The Good News has reached us, and it couldn't be better! The Son of God has died for us; he loves us that much. That Son of God who died for us rose from the dead and is with us right here and now, and he will never leave us.

This Jesus, from whose love no power can separate us, is busy teaching us, healing us, forgiving us, and doing everything that needs doing in order to bring us safely home to

God our Father. He gives all that is his to give so that we might become heirs with him to the eternal joys of paradise.

This is the Good News, and there is no piece of news more essential to the happiness and holiness of the entire world.

Isn't it amazing? Salvation has come, and by some strange and wonderful plan of God, we are its messengers! We would feel so flattered if a king or queen or president or head of a large corporation sent us as a personal messenger to carry good news to a far-off nation. We have been sent by God himself with the best message ever communicated, and our job is to carry that news not to a particular nation, but to every creature and country of the entire world.

These words of the great prophet Isaiah are as beautiful as any poem, and refer in a powerful and persuasive way to our own evangelistic mission:

For as the rain and the snow come down from heaven,
and do not return there

until they have watered the earth,
making it bring forth and sprout,
giving seed to the sower
and bread to the eater,
so shall my word be
that goes out from my mouth;
it shall not return to me empty,
but it shall accomplish
that which I purpose,
and succeed in the thing for which I sent it.
(Isaiah 55:10-11)

God has spoken his Word, the living Word of Life we call Jesus Christ. We have heard this Word. It is the answer to our every need. It is a Word that cannot and will not be wasted. It will accomplish everything that the Father has sent it to do. It will bring home to heaven every one of the chosen and adopted sons and daughters of God.

For us, what a glorious act of kindness, what an enthralling mission, what a privilege and joy to be an evangelizer, shouting from the housetops the Good News that Jesus Christ is our Friend and Brother, our Savior and Shepherd, our Lord, God, and King!

This job is ours, and if we are true Christians, worthy of our baptism, we will be busy doing the job, and doing it well, from one end of the earth to the other! n

Chapter 3

How to Evangelize

I keep running around the world proclaiming to everyone I can that evangelization is the job God gave to all Christians, emphasizing that it is a job that must be done, and done well. Again and again the question comes back: "But *how* do I do it? How can I evangelize effectively, and in ways that open others to the life in abundance promised by our Lord?"

Do parents just command little children to bend down and tie their own shoelaces? That would be unkind. No, the parents themselves bend to patiently and gently teach their little children how to tie those shoelaces. In the same way, it is not fair for me to be telling people about their obligation to evangelize without giving some answers to that often-asked question, "*How* do I evangelize?" Together with informing people of their obligations, we need to offer some practical advice on how to do the job.

Not Just a Question of Technique

When we move into this area of how to evangelize, people are usually looking for answers that spell out some very clever techniques, or they want to be handed a detailed program that is easy to follow step by step. For example, I met a charming woman in the Virgin Islands who was wearing one of those watches that comes with a variety of interchangeable and multicolored watch straps. When I looked at her wrist, I saw the watch straps, but no watch. I said to the woman with concern, "Whoops! It looks like you may have lost your watch." She greeted those words with one of those glorious Caribbean smiles, delighted that I was falling into her trap. "It's all right," she said with an even brighter smile, "I already know that *now's the time*." Then she just sat there, smiling and waiting for me to tumble into the next level of her holy snare by naively asking, "Time for what?" As soon as anyone said that, she could start bubbling out the Good News: "Time for getting to know Jesus!"

Now that joyful little technique worked perfectly for her, because it fit so well into her playful Caribbean character and culture. The same can be said of any number of techniques and programs that work well for the right people in the right parts of the world. The fact is, though, that all techniques and programs must be *encultured*, and that means sensitively accommodated to the personalities, circumstances, and environments of the particular people evangelizing and being evangelized. The same styles and methods don't necessarily work that well for everyone everywhere.

Acknowledging that point, suppose a young boy wanted to learn how to play basketball and could receive lessons from anyone he wished. Whom would he pick to be his teacher? I've asked that question on a hundred different occasions, and every time the same answer comes roaring back: "Michael Jordan!" In other words, we want to learn from the pro, the one with the reputation of playing the game better than anyone else in the world.

Well then, who are the outstanding "pros" of history in the life-enriching task of evangelization? In the entire

history of the Church, who were the greatest of all evangelizers, including the likes of Patrick and Francis Xavier? Putting aside our Blessed Mother Mary, who is in a special category all her own, the three greatest of all carriers of the Good News are heroic St. John the Baptist, the eloquent apostle St. Paul, and of course Jesus, the Word himself.

Who are the outstanding "pros" of history in the life-enriching task of evangelization?

So, rather than offering a list of optional styles and techniques, here are nine grace-filled attitudes exemplified by these three great pros that can succeed in enlightening and transforming us to the point of becoming fully competent for our mission. But first, a brief look at our three experts themselves:

JOHN THE BAPTIST: Scripture calls John the Baptist "a prophet and more than a prophet," while Jesus singled him out as the greatest "among those born of women" (Luke 7:26,28). In the Gospel, he is described as "The voice of one crying out in the wilderness: 'Prepare the way of the Lord, make his paths straight' " (Matthew 3:3). By listing him among the greatest of all evangelizers, we are indicating that when he shared the Good News, the people and the whole society around him were changed. As Matthew describes it, his words made things happen. "The people of Jerusalem and all Judea were going out to him, and all the region along the Jordan, and they were baptized by him in the river Jordan, confessing their sins" (Matthew 3:5-6). In other words, when John evangelized, streets were deserted and whole towns emptied out as multitudes headed into the desert to hang upon his words, confess their sins, and hand over their lives to God. John was an evangelizer, and he was definitely good at doing the job.

SAINT PAUL: Jesus described Saul, who was to become St. Paul, with these words, "He is a chosen instrument of mine to carry my name before the Gentiles and kings and the sons of Israel" (Acts 9:15). We read in the Acts of the Apostles that even his enemies rated Paul as someone who was turning the whole world upside down, his sermons at times triggering even riots in the streets (Acts 17:6; 19:23). The secular magazine *National Geographic* produced a beautiful book called *Bible Times*. The last chapter of that book, entitled "The World of Paul," describes the effects of Paul's proclamations with these words: He "had an impact on history, second only to the birth of Christ." He "changed the course of Christianity, and with it the course of the world. . . . His epistles to his congregations, letters which rank next to the words of Jesus in spiritual power, reveal him as Christianity's most creative exponent" (pages 379, 381). He was the great missionary whose Good News changed the world.

Only one evangelizer could possibly be even more effective than that, and that one person, of course, is Jesus himself.

JESUS CHRIST: Scripture describes our Lord as "a prophet mighty in deed and word before God and all the people" (Luke 24:19). He was certainly that, and so much more! He proclaimed God's word, and he is the Word. For us, he is God's messenger and the life-giving message God sent. He was anointed by the Holy Spirit to proclaim Good News to the poor, and he is the Good News. He began to preach when still only a small boy, and even the priests and doctors in the temple listened to his words with admiration. Officials and ordinary people cried out, "No man ever spoke like this man!" (John 7:46). His Sermon on the Mount is undoubtedly the greatest sermon ever preached; even pagans repeat his words without knowing whom they are quoting. He evangelized in synagogues, on street corners, and in marketplaces. He preached on mountaintops and in remote desert places. He stood in a small boat and preached to great crowds lining the shore and to one wayward woman at a well. Multitudes gathered to hear him, but he still found time to bless and embrace the little children.

We realize how powerful his words were when we read that when he spoke to the dead, even they listened and obeyed and came back to life. As he hung dying his anguishing death on the cross, he was busy proclaiming his life-giving seven last words; and after he came back from the dead, he went on for another forty days preaching, teaching, and evangelizing before returning in glory to his heavenly Father. Standing there at the throne of God, he then sent us the Holy Spirit so that we could be empowered to continue his mission by being his witnesses to the ends of the earth.

Evangelii Nuntiandi, Pope Paul VI's great apostolic letter on evangelization which I've heard several non-Catholic pastors call the finest document ever written on the subject, states enthusiastically that "Jesus himself, the Good News of God, was the very first and the greatest evangelizer" (7).

Nine Attitudes of Highly Successful Evangelizers

Jesus tells us that the corn is ripe and the harvest is great. He urges us to beg God to send needed laborers into the fields. So let's take a practical look at these three great evangelizers to see how we, too, can be included among the number of those working effectively to carry the Good News to the farthest corners of the earth, and most especially into the hearts and lives of our own dear relatives, friends, neighbors, and acquaintances.

As exemplified by John the Baptist, the Apostle Paul, and of course Jesus himself, our *Wisdom from God*

(1 Corinthians 1:30), let's study the following nine attitudes that can transform us into dynamically effective and successful evangelizers.

1. Have the mind of someone chosen and sent by God.

When John the Evangelist introduces the Baptist to us in the first words of his Gospel, he describes him with these words: "There was a man *sent* from God, whose name was John" (John 1:6). St. Paul, in turn, introduces himself to us with these words: "Paul, a servant of Jesus Christ, called to be an apostle, set apart for the gospel of God" (Romans 1:1). He offers a similar resume in the opening words of his letter to the Galatians, where we read, "Paul an apostle—not from men nor through man, but through Jesus Christ and God the Father, who raised him from the dead . . . who had set me apart before I was born, and had called me through his grace" (Galatians 1:1,15). It was Ananias who first enlightened Paul about his God-given mission by telling him, "The God of our fathers appointed you to know his will . . . you will be a witness for him to all men" (Acts 22:14-15), an understanding made crystal clear to Paul by Jesus himself, who commissioned him by saying, "I will *send* you . . . to the Gentiles" (22:21).

Not only John and Paul but Jesus, too, knew and clearly understood that God had sent him. I could count in the pages of Scripture the number of places where Jesus is quoted as saying that he was "sent by the Father," but no one knows exactly how many times and in how many ways he emphasized this important truth to his disciples and listeners. Clearly, it was vitally important to him that others understood that God had sent him.

After making this known, Jesus in turns tells us in the clearest words, "You did not choose me, but I chose you and appointed you that you should go and bear fruit. . . . As the Father sent me, even so I send you" (John 15:16; 20:21).

This realization of being chosen and sent by God transforms us into capable evangelizers in two ways. First of all, the understanding that we are being sent by God himself makes us face the fact that there is no getting out of the job. When a king sends a servant, when the pope sends a priest, when a president sends his ambassador, or when the head of a corporation sends a worker, the one commissioned loses his options. The authority in the voice of the one sending him makes it clear that he must go. The one who sends us is more than a bank president or office boss. He is our Creator and God, and that ends *our* options. One well-known figure in the Bible tried to hold onto his options after being sent by God to a town called Nineveh. Jonah realized his mistake only after God sent a whale to set him back on track. It is just possible that there may be a whale with his mouth wide open snapping at our heels right behind us.

The second transformation that comes from seeing ourselves as chosen and sent by God is the way we speak the message entrusted to us. When a king, a

When we speak, people should hear the authority of Christ in our tone of voice and in the conviction with which we proclaim and believe the message.

president, or a prime minister sends an ambassador, the person sent speaks with the authority of the one who sent him. Ambassadors of Christ (2 Corinthians 5:20) speak with unhesitating confidence because they are echoing the voice of him who spoke with greater authority than anyone else who ever spoke (cf. Luke 4:32). When we speak, people should hear the authority of Christ in our tone of voice and in the conviction with which we proclaim and believe the message.

John, Paul, and Jesus never doubted for a moment that they had been chosen and sent by God, and for that reason alone they spoke God's word, and spoke it in a way that echoed the authority of God himself.

2. Always speak with humility. This second attitude balances the first, and is the incredibly important secret to true spiritual power for the task of leading others to Christ. Evangelizers must not be proud!

John the Baptist was great in humility, declaring flatly that he was not the Messiah, belittling himself to the point of stating that he was unfit even to carry the Messiah's sandals (Matthew 3:11). His humility carried him even further. When he saw people continuing to confuse his qualities with the incomparable greatness of Jesus himself, he made the prophetic statement, "He must increase, but I must decrease" (John 3:30). With those words, he was foreseeing his imminent death. He would soon decrease quickly and very decisively by having his head chopped off, and in that way, he would no longer distract others from recognizing Jesus as the true and only Messiah.

St. Paul was a brilliant and highly educated man, but he saw all of his limitations, declaring that he would brag only of his weakness so that Christ could be powerful in him (2 Corinthians 12:9-10). With these words, Paul was pointing clearly to the secret of spiritual power. If I think myself strong, I will be trying to do for others what I can do for them. If I believe myself wise, I will share with them my own tiny bits of wisdom. If I see myself as rich and powerful, I will give others what little I have to give. The fact is that I don't have nearly enough strength, wisdom, and riches even for myself. Only by accepting my own weakness and frailty can I do the real job of sharing with the world

Jesus gave all the glory and credit for his good works to the Father who sent him. everything that Christ has done and won for us, communicating all that Christ can give us.

Paul sums up this thought with the empowering words, "I planted, Apollos watered, but God gave the growth. So neither he who plants nor he who waters is anything, but only God who gives the growth" (1 Corinthians 3:6-7). Whenever I repeat these words in talks, I always paraphrase the quotation a bit by saying, "I plant—so what; Apollos waters—no big deal. The only one who matters is God himself, who alone makes the seed grow and bear fruit in abundance."

What about the humility of Jesus? When instructing us to learn from him, he could have pointed to his prayerfulness, kindness, purity, obedience, or any of the other great virtues he practiced to perfection. In telling us to learn from him, the quality he singled was the empowering virtue of humility: "Learn from me; for I am gentle and humble in heart" (Matthew 11:29). Because he was humble, Jesus gave all the glory and credit for his good works to the Father who sent him (John 14:13).

Calling themselves evangelizers, some print their own names in large letters on big banners, proclaiming themselves even to be "miracle workers." Whatever they can work is no real miracle, since the word "miracle" means actions that only God can perform. To the degree that any evangelizer focuses on himself rather than exclusively upon God, he loses his spiritual power.

Emphasizing this point, St. Peter writes: "Whoever speaks must do so as one speaking the very words of God; whoever serves must do so with the strength that God supplies, so that God may be glorified in all things through Jesus Christ" (1 Peter 4:11). Isaiah the prophet expresses this same thought with these words, "Shall the ax vaunt itself over the one who wields it, or the saw magnify itself against the one who handles it?" (Isaiah 10:15). When we see ourselves as nothing more than tools in the hands of God, our actions have power! By giving all of the glory to God, we are giving God visibility in his world, and that's an excellent definition of evangelization.

If anyone asked about my ambition in life, I could playfully—yet very seriously—respond that I wouldn't mind being "a piece of plastic tube in the hands of God." I don't want the tube to be made of silver or gold, because those precious metals can draw attention to themselves. Plastic tubing would be just fine, provided that through it could freely pass "the waters of life."

3. Proclaim only the Word. College professors, successful business owners, philosophers, and medical experts have many important and helpful things to say and teach. Seriously written books and scientific articles also contain essential wisdom as the fruit of serious study, experimentation, and discovery. All of this is essential to our human progress, but communicating these truths is not what we call evangelization. A message of divine wisdom, a living Word, was sent from God, and the communication of that Word, referring to Jesus himself, is exactly what we call evangelization.

We read that John the Baptist "was not the light, but he came to testify to the light" (John 1:8). St. Paul declares decisively that he would "not venture to speak of anything except what Christ has accomplished" (Romans 15:18). Anyone spending most of his time talking about his own ideas and accomplishments or just quoting himself doesn't meet the qualifications of an authentic evangelizer.

Along these lines, Jesus makes a startling statement that should receive full attention from some modern scholars who, at times, seem to be coming up with new doctrines of their own while watering down some of our oldest convictions. Referring to his own instructions, Jesus tells us: "My teaching is not mine but his who sent me" (John 7:16). If Jesus Christ dares to proclaim only and exactly what his heavenly Father sent him to reveal, all of us should be extremely careful to do exactly that and nothing more.

Summing it up, an evangelizer's only job is to proclaim Jesus Christ, the living Word of God. "For we do not proclaim ourselves; we proclaim Jesus Christ as Lord and ourselves as your slaves for Jesus' sake" (2 Corinthians 4:5). We hear Catholics around the world complaining that they are not satisfied with some of the Sunday homilies they hear, which indicates not only a hunger for the nourishing Word of God but also that many are underfed.

I sometimes play a little trick on an audience by telling them to take out their Bibles "and open to St. Paul's letter to the Athenians." Despite a forewarning, some still fall into the trap and immediately start flipping pages. St. Paul visited Rome, and we have his letter to the Romans. He went to Corinth, and the Bible contains his two letters to that city. It was the same with other cities that he visited: Galatia, Ephesus, Philippi, and so on. We read in the Acts of the Apostles that he also went to Athens, debating with their scholars and philosophers in the Areopagus (Acts 17:22). In the Bible, though, we find no Pauline letter to the Athenians. In Athens alone, Paul seems to toss a mixed salad of pagan philosophies, false gods, and human thinking together with the wonders of revealed truth, and only in Athens did he fail to leave behind a blossoming Christian community to whom he would write back. After that he never tossed another mixed salad, devoting his teachings instead to the rich red meat of Christ's words, example, and salvific actions.

. There is no reason to criticize others for teaching valid and useful human truths, but in the words of Paul, "As for you, teach what is consistent with sound doctrine" (Titus 2:1). It is as straightforward and simple as this: "Hear and believe in the Word of God! I live the

Everyone who believes that Christ transmits the Word of Eternal Life must witness to his or her belief by living that Word.

Word, and it gives me abundant life. Live that Word and you too will have life in abundance."

4. Witness to the Word you proclaim. It would be a little too easy if evangelizers did nothing more than speak words. Speakers lose credibility when they mouth the words without living them. Everyone who believes that Christ transmits the Word of Eternal Life must witness to his or her belief by living that Word, and living it to the hilt. In other words, we have to do more than proclaim the Good News. We must show the world how good it is by the joy with which we live it. The sound of truth must be in our voices, and the proof must be in our lives.

John the Baptist preached a life of penance. This is why we do not read in the story of his life that he ate three banquets a day in the best restaurants, or dressed himself in the purple robes of royalty, or lived in a luxurious palace or castle. No, he called the world to repent, and his whole life was an act of penance. For food, he satisfied himself with locusts and wild honey. He dressed in the rough and hard skins of camels, and his home was the barren desert. He was credible enough to draw whole cities out into that parched desert, because people saw him doing everything he called them to do.

In Philippians 3:17, Paul tells us to follow him just as he follows Christ. In a second translation of the same text, he calls us to imitate him in the way he imitates Jesus. A third, and my own favorite translation, has him inviting us to be his disciples in the way that he is a true disciple of Jesus Christ. No matter which of the three translations we prefer, the clear message is that Paul is free to tell us that he is doing everything he urges us to do. We can learn from Paul's example how to live as Christians because we see Paul living the life of Christ. He is not just a talker but also a true witness to the value and truth of Christ's message. He is so convinced of what he says that he has made it his life.

And what about Jesus himself? In his wondrous Sermon on the Mount, he instructs us to do many difficult things. We are told to turn the other cheek, love our enemies, and forgive those who do us harm. Not one of these commands does he fail to obey himself. As a matter of fact, he asks nothing of us that we do not see him doing to perfection. That's why he tells us, "Learn from me!" (Matthew 11:29). He never points a finger telling us to go while standing perfectly still himself. He is the first one on the go, moving decisively toward the heights he lays out for us. Only then does he turn to us with the encouraging words, "Come, follow me" (19:21).

Every evangelizer must be a true believer, and this means that he must be so convinced of what he is saying that it becomes the truth he lives. David du Plessis, a good friend, a true ecumenist, and an excellent Pentecostal preacher, was always ready with pithy spiritual sound bytes rich in truth. To bring out the need for all evangelizers to be witnesses, he simply stated: "If we were saltier, the whole world would be thirstier." Others would be enjoying the full flavor of the Good News much more quickly if we ourselves were more seasoned in it.

5. Be courageous. This quality, seen to such an extraordinary degree in the lives of John, Paul, and Jesus, is an important lesson for Catholics today. Among the Christians of the world, Catholics—especially those of the affluent West—remain extremely shy about expressing their faith or making any kind of spiritual sound. Because John and Paul spoke out so boldly, both of them were beheaded. Because Jesus proclaimed the truth, he was nailed to a cross.

The early Christians followed Jesus' example. We read in chapter four of the Acts of the Apostles that when Peter and John were beaten and threatened with a worse fate if they ever mentioned the name of Jesus again, the community of early Christians gathered to pray, and their prayer was not, "Dear Lord, save us from the cops!" Rather, they prayed: "Now Lord . . . grant to your servants to speak your word with all boldness" (Acts 4:29). When they finished the prayer, the Holy Spirit was poured down upon them with a power that shook the whole building where they were praying, and from that moment on, "they were all filled with the

Holy Spirit and spoke the word of God with boldness," and "with great power the apostles gave their testimony to the resurrection of the Lord Jesus, and great grace was upon them all" (4:31-33).

I could not love or admire St. Paul more than I do. Even so, if I ever had the chance to do so before a large audience, I would willingly embarrass him. Explaining to him how much I loved that crowd and knowing that he too loved them, I would ask him to turn toward the wall behind him and remove his shirt. Were Paul to do so, I know exactly what that whole crowd would do. With one voice, every one of them would let out a deep gasp and a groan of horrified astonishment, saying, "Never could I have imagined or expected to see anything like that." In ancient Roman times, medical experts estimated that forty strokes of the lash were capable of killing a man. For that reason, Roman law determined that only prisoners condemned to death could be given the full forty lashes. All others could be sentenced only to "forty strokes, less one." Paul was given that punishment no less than five times, then three more times with rods, and another time with rocks. Who can come close to imagining what his back looked like? Yet nothing deterred or frightened him from continuing courageously with his task of carrying the Good News to pagans, governors, and kings.

When Valerian D'Souza, Bishop of Poona, India, spoke at the second Worldwide Retreat for Priests, he told the story of young Catholic men evangelizing tribes of

> **We seem to be waiting for that perfectly safe and trouble-free moment before beginning to evangelize.**

Animists in the Himalayan foothills of northern India. The boys found themselves attacked by a group of Hindu fundamentalists who beat them so severely that some were left with broken arms and legs, while others had their mouths stuffed with cow dung taken from the streets. The boys had to go back into the cities, where they were cleaned up and given needed medical attention. As soon as they were back on their feet, and with a courage that can only leave us in admiration, they turned around and headed back to the mountains to complete the job of bringing the Good News to those open and attentive mountain people.

Despite such stories of heroism, we western Catholics can fear making the sign of the cross before beginning a restaurant meal and be timid about mentioning Christ even to our own children and closest friends because someone might reject us with a look or critical word. We seem to be waiting for that perfectly safe and trouble-free moment before beginning to evangelize. I heard a speaker once say that "if Jesus had waited for a perfectly safe moment before coming to save us, we would still be waiting for him to appear, and in fact he would never arrive." Our Lord warned that the task of proclaiming the "stone rejected" would lead us in turn to be rejected (Acts 4:11). If we have never experienced any kind of persecution, it may indicate that we have never evangelized in a bold enough way. Jesus instructed us to take up his cross and follow him, and that means that the job was never meant to be easy. It is a mission that definitely calls for courage.

6. Depend upon the power of the Holy Spirit. The task is clearly a supernatural one. Building the kingdom of God by spreading the Good News of Jesus Christ requires divine power, and the name of the One who is that power is the Holy Spirit. John the Baptist received the Holy Spirit's power while still in his mother's womb; even before his own birth, he was enabled to announce the Messiah's arrival by jumping for joy as Mary, pregnant with Jesus, entered the home of Elizabeth (Luke 1:15,41,44).

When Ananias laid hands on him, Paul received the Holy Spirit, together with all the power needed for making Christ known to governors and kings and, amazingly for him as a very orthodox Hebrew, even to the Gentiles (Acts 9:17). This divine power made Paul so successful that, as already quoted, *National Geographic* described him as having "changed the course of Christianity, and with it the course of the world."

In his humanity, Jesus too received the Holy Spirit's outpouring of divine power. After he humbly descended into the waters of the Jordan to receive the baptism of John, the Holy Spirit descended upon him in the form of a dove

(Matthew 3:16). It was from that moment on that he went forward in power and began to win admiration from the people for his wisdom and authority and the magnificence of his teachings.

Christ promised to send his Holy Spirit as a "power from on high" that would remind us of all that he had taught and done (Luke 24:49; John 14:26). He assured us that when taken before governors and kings, it would not be we who spoke but rather the Spirit speaking through us and making us effective witnesses of Jesus to the ends of the earth (Matthew 10:18; Mark 13:9; Acts 1:8). Our voices produce sound waves that reach the eardrums of listeners. Only the Holy Spirit can take those words and carry them into hearts and minds with a power capable of bringing about someone's total transformation.

When we see how Jesus, Mary, John the Baptist, Peter, and Paul, the greatest figures of Christian history, were all in need of the power of the Holy Spirit in order to fulfill their mission, we would certainly be arrogant and seriously mistaken if we decided that we could do the job completely on our own. Salvation is a work of God, and that means that only God can do the job while freely using us through the power of his Holy Spirit. It's that simple!

7. Give time to prayer and preparation. People today understand that to succeed in a profession and to have a good income, they must study and work hard. Before beginning their public lives, both Jesus and John did this for a full thirty years. Paul did something similar by studying at the feet of the scholar Gamaliel (Acts 22:3). I've heard some people announce that they had not carefully prepared a talk they were about to give, "because I want to leave room for the Holy Spirit to freely speak through me." They seem to be saying that the Holy Spirit can speak to and through them only if they already have a river of words flowing from their open mouths. The Spirit speaks much better and is heard more clearly when our lips are shut in preparatory study and prayer.

Regarding prayer, it seems that the whole life of John the Baptist was a time of penance and prayer. Paul, in turn, carried on a continuous prayer campaign, not only by praying constantly himself, but also by ending almost all of his epistles with requests for the prayers of others: "Pray also for me, so that when I speak, a message may be given to me to make known with boldness the mystery of the gospel" (Ephesians 6:19). "Pray for us as well that God will open to us a door for the word . . . so that I may reveal it clearly, as I should" (Colossians 4:3-4). "Pray for us, so that the word of the Lord may spread rapidly and be glorified everywhere" (2 Thessalonians 3:1).

No one had a busier life than Jesus himself. He traveled the roads of Galilee constantly, met everywhere by crowds yearning to hear his word and beg a blessing. With all of the excitement surrounding him, he never made prayer an option, even on the busiest days. "In the morning, while it was still very dark, he got up and went out to

If, in a week that always contains 168 hours, we can never find time for prayerfully studying God's Word, we have to start thinking that our lives are seriously out of order.

a deserted place, and there he prayed" (Mark 1:35). Again and again we see him speaking to his heavenly Father. Especially before making any of the most important decisions of his life, we find him deep in prayer. We read of him doing so just before choosing his twelve apostles (Luke 6:12); before promising his body and blood as food and drink (John 6:15); prior to making Peter prince of the apostles (Matthew 16:18); and of course during his agony in the Garden in preparation for his death on the cross (Matthew 26:36).

Evangelization is the mission of speaking *to* others about God. How can anyone do that in ways that are effective and interesting, if they never take time or show any interest in speaking *with* God?

St. Augustine dedicated a great part of his life to opposing the Pelagian heresy. Pelagius denied the supernatural, claiming that there was an innate perfection hidden within us that can be released through our own human efforts. In other words, man can save himself! Anyone attempting to lead others to perfection, anyone attempting to evangelize without doing so prayerfully is a Pelagian by implication. Our perfection and sanctification is undeniably a work of God and therefore can be accomplished only by the graces we receive though prayer.

Nothing takes priority over nourishing the People of God with the Word of God. To do this well, we must be students of the Word. There are people who say they would love to read the Bible but can't find the time. They have time to read the newspapers and *People Magazine*, and they spend dozens of hours each week channel surfing the TV in a frustrated hope of finding something worth watching. If, in a week that always contains 168 hours, we can never find time for prayerfully studying God's Word, we have to start thinking that our lives are seriously out of order. We prioritize less important activities and give low priority to acquiring the greatest truths by failing to focus time and effort on the healing and sanctifying Word of God.

If this is a mistake in general, it is an especially big one for those who stand before others to speak about God, and who attempt to help others understand the life and teachings of Christ. St. Francis of Assisi was not an ordained priest but rather a humble monk who held priests in awe and respect. Yet he never hesitated to point out that "an ignorant preacher is more dangerous than sin!" That warning applies equally to evangelizers. Their mission is to make Christ known, and to do that well they must *know* Christ well. They must be students of his salvific plan and have his words of healing at the tip of their tongues. To someone saddened and burdened, they must be ready to echo the words,

"Come to me, all you that are weary" (Matthew 11:28). For someone lonely and feeling depressed, the words of Christ that can help are, "Remember, I am with you always, to the end of the age" (Matthew 28:20). To someone reaching the end of his life, the words that can encourage and console are, "Everyone who lives and believes in me will never die" (John 11:26).

To support and strengthen others at difficult moments, to bring hope and joy in times of sadness and sickness, or just to brighten a cloudy day, there is nothing more effective than God's own words, which carry so much wisdom, light, and strength. I don't know how many times I've been able to console anguished parents of a wayward son or daughter who no longer practices the faith or who is lost to an addiction or in a bad relationship by telling them that they planted good seeds in the heart of their child and can now pray for their child with absolute confidence on the basis of this divine promise: "If anyone sees his brother commit a sin . . . he has only to pray, and God will give life to this brother" (1 John 5:16, NJB). It is amazing to see how much help can be transmitted by speaking God's Word in the right way and at the right time, but to speak convincingly, we must stay in contact with the Word of God through prayer and study.

In different Christian cultures around the world—Irish, Spanish, and Italian, for example—there are all kinds of beautiful phrases, blessings, greetings, and wishes that communicate faith, hope, and love. Words and phrases like these, when taken from the pages of Scripture, can at times prove more effective than even the wise counsel of the best psychologists. They are God's own words, and study and prayer can put them on our lips.

8. Seek and expect signs and wonders. Here again is an attitude and an ideal that comes as a surprise to many Catholics. In the concluding words of Mark's Gospel, we hear Jesus making this promise: "Go into all the world and proclaim the good news to the whole creation. . . . These signs will accompany those who believe: by using my name they will cast out demons; they will speak in new tongues; they will pick up snakes in their hands, and if they drink any deadly thing, it will not hurt them; they will lay their hands on the sick, and they will recover." We then read that "they went out and proclaimed the good news everywhere, while the Lord worked with them and confirmed the message by the signs that accompanied it" (Mark 16:15-20).

John the Baptist was a penniless preacher wandering barefoot through the desert, yet the strength of his holiness frightened even powerful and brutal King Herod (Mark 6:20). When Paul was unable to visit someone who was ill, he sent a disciple to touch the person with his handkerchief and in that way bring healing and help to the sick person (Acts 19:11-12). When enemies doubted Christ and set traps to destroy him, he told them that though they failed to believe in his words,

We are told that if we had faith like a grain of mustard seed, we could uproot mountains of sin, sickness, hatred, and injustice, and cast them into the sea. they should be convinced by the wondrous works they saw him performing (John 10:38; Acts 10:38). If signs and wonders were necessary for Jesus and for Christian heroes as great as the John the Baptist and St. Paul, how much more are they needed by us?

Not only are they needed; they are expected! There is decisiveness in the way Jesus tells us, "Very truly, I tell you, the one who believes in me will also do the works that I do and, in fact, will do greater works than these" (John 14:12). He grows impatient when Peter fails to walk confidently on water (Matthew 14:31) and is deeply disappointed when the apostles do nothing to help the father of the boy with epilepsy (Luke 9:41).

Blithely telling people that Jesus loves us and can help us without ever calling upon him to do so is not convincing. Because the devil is so powerful in today's world, dominating as he does all the modern means of communication, we need to see some demonstrations of the greater power of God, along the lines of Elijah in competitive battle with the priests of Baal (1 Kings 18:20-40) or Mary occasioning a spectacular miracle at the wedding feast of Cana (John 2:1-11).

We are told that if we had faith like a grain of mustard seed, we could uproot mountains of sin, sickness, hatred, and injustice, and cast them into the sea (Mark 11:23; Matthew 17:20; Luke 17:5-6). The world needs to see some good things actually happening, and that means God wants us to be praying expectantly for signs and wonders.

9. Sound joyful and optimistic. The word "Gospel" means Good News, and one of the jobs of evangelizers is to make that news sound good. Cynical comedians sometimes mimic preachers by portraying them as always speaking with thunderous but depressing doomsday cadences. Is that the way our three greatest evangelizers cried out the Good News?

I hear only delight in the voice of John the Baptist as he called out, "Behold, the Lamb of God, who takes away the sin of the world!" (John 1:29). John lived his whole life to reach that moment of joy when Christ stood before him, ready to be made known to the multitudes. I see John leaping with exuberance as he spoke those words that were the most joyful piece of news anyone has ever announced.

Paul lists joy among the precious fruits of the Holy Spirit (Galatians 5:22), and speaks constantly about the joy he takes in his brother and sister Christians (Romans 15:24,32; Philippians 4:1; 1 Thessalonians 3:9). He is such an optimist that he gives us the assurance that "all things work together for good for those who love God" (Romans 8:28).

The angel was not chanting a dirge when, at the birth of Christ, he sang out, "Good news of great joy for all the people" (Luke 2:10). Those crowds of thousands that followed Jesus into the desert and climbed into trees and up mountaintops just to get a glimpse of him were not expecting to hear sad stories. Jesus announced at the very beginning of his public life that he had been anointed by the Holy Spirit "to bring glad news to the poor" (Luke 4:18). And that is exactly what he brought!

No doomsday prophet is an evangelizer! Evangelizers announce that in Jesus Christ we have the pearl of greatest price, the hidden treasure more valuable than anything else. He is the God who loves us enough to die for us, the King who shares with us all the riches of his kingdom!

That Good News is good, and yet I have heard announcers on television proclaiming a new brand of soap with more joy and enthusiasm than we sometimes hear from Sunday pulpits. Since the Jubilee Year 2000, a young priest in Brazil is gathering tens of thousands for weekday Masses and hundreds of thousands for religious gatherings in large soccer stadiums. When the television program *20/20* aired a documentary about him, I tried to analyze what makes the priest so attractive and concluded that it is his joy.

The world paints religion as dull, drab, and depriving. It is the exact opposite: our surest road to peace and joy! If our words and actions bubble with optimistic hope and pleasure, if our talk is happy and if our faces smile, the world will start to see that Jesus truly *is* Good News.

Ordinary Opportunities for Proclaiming the Good News

It is important to show here how easy it is to evangelize once we make these nine essential attitudes our own. I try to do this by asking audiences when was the last time that someone mentioned to them some problem, pain, or fear. It could have been a headache, stomachache, or heartache. It could have been a husband drinking too much, a son no longer going to church, or a daughter living with a boyfriend. It could have been a money problem or a bout of nervousness or depression. Perhaps the doctor gave them some bad news about their health. Maybe it was a bit of tension or an argument that hasn't been resolved. Whenever I ask people how long it's been since they had such a conversation, the usual answer is either "Just this morning" or "Yesterday afternoon."

No matter how the person expressed their problem, I can accurately translate what they were saying in these words: "I am looking for the person or thing that can *save* me from this problem. I went to the doctor, the banker, the lawyer, and the politician, and I've even visited the psychiatrist. None of them has yet saved me from my problem, so I am still looking for someone who can do it."

Now when someone comes to you with that kind of a difficulty, what do you say? A not uncommon response is to say something like this: "You think you've got problems!" Then you start adding your problems to

The next time someone mentions a problem, just say: "You know, I have had problems just like that, and I always take them to Jesus."

theirs. For example, they inform you they may need an operation, and you start saying, "Let me tell you about my operation!" Now, what kind of help is that? They came to you with one operation on their mind, and now they have two to worry about!

Instead of doubling their worries, why not hear exactly what they are saying, though perhaps not exactly in these words: "I am searching for whom or what can save me from this problem!" The fact that they expressed this need to you is the result of a direct action of the Holy Spirit, giving you a perfect opportunity for proclaiming the name of the *One Who Saves*. It's that simple, and occasions for doing it occur almost every day of your life!

So the next time someone mentions a problem, just say: "You know, I have had problems just like that, and I always take them to Jesus. He is there for me every time, consoling and strengthening me and giving me courage and wisdom and patience to await an answer. He always gets me through it, and he loves you just as much as he loves me. So he is there for you, too."

And then it's time to say something that requires just a bit more courage: "So let me say a little prayer for you." Then taking them by the hand or laying your hand on their shoulder or head, say a short prayer of faith, asking Jesus to be the answer to their problem and all their needs.

That's it! You did the job! You just evangelized! God gave you the opportunity and you made good use of it, first of all by naming the One who saves, and then with your prayer, handing them over to Jesus the Savior. Your job is done. Now it's all up to Jesus, and there's no reason to doubt that he in turn will do his job, and do it well!

Summing it all up, the Savior of the world has come. His name is Jesus of Nazareth. Amazingly, God has chosen and sent us to be his witnesses. Our mission is to make him known. We must proclaim him as the Word of Life humbly, so that he himself can work powerfully in and through us. But we must do more than simply proclaim the Word. We must live it in ways that make us true witnesses of Jesus Christ to the very ends of the earth. We must be dedicated men and women of study and prayer who act courageously and depend totally and explicitly upon the power of the Holy Spirit, expecting and experiencing signs and wonders, as God works through us in ways that fill us with hope and optimism and unconquerable joy!

Yes, the Good News is good, and for those who know how to proclaim it, life just couldn't be better. n

Chapter 4

Knowing the Christ We Proclaim

I once gave away a million dollars. Do you believe me? The more exact truth is that I gave away a million dollars not once but twice, and the second time the amount was closer to a million and a half dollars. How about it? Do you believe me now?

I can't waste your time telling lies, and I certainly don't write down lies in the pages of a book. So both these statements are true. The first time I gave away the million was on the occasion of the First Worldwide Retreat for Priests at Vatican City in 1984. The million-and-a-half dollars were distributed in preparation for the Second Worldwide Retreat for Priests in 1990. We wanted both these retreats to be *worldwide* in fact, not simply in name. This meant that we didn't want priests to attend only from the United States and the more affluent countries of Western Europe. We wanted poorer priests to be there from the *campos* of Latin America, from the bush of Africa, from tiny islands of the Pacific, and from the ice of Siberia. So I distributed the millions in order to give them a chance to participate.

Before I gave away the money, there was something very important that I first had to do. I had to meet and get to know the man who had the millions to give me, so that I could give them away. Now, go back a few sentences and recheck that. I never said that the millions I gave were mine. I only said that I gave them away, and that was easy enough to do once I met that multimillionaire and his dear wife, who offered me the money even before I dreamed of asking for it.

God has called us all to be evangelizers, and evangelizers give away far more than a mere million dollars.

Evangelizers give away the pearl of greatest price, and the price of that pearl is so great that only Jesus can pay it. Evangelizers give away the hidden treasure worth more than everything else the world contains, and Jesus Christ is the only way that leads us to that treasure. Evangelizers give away paradise, but only Jesus has and is the key that opens for us the gates of paradise by speaking to us his words of eternal life. Evangelizers give away eternal salvation, but Jesus is the only name given to man by which he is to be saved. Only Jesus is the spotless Lamb who washes away all of our sins.

So it stands to reason that in the same way that I first had to meet and come to know that wonderful man in Holland before I could give away the millions, evangelizers must first come to know Jesus Christ before they can help distribute the riches he won for us by his life, death, and resurrection. In Eucharistic celebrations we proclaim again and again that from him come all good things. How can we share those good things with others unless we first make contact with their source?

Recognizing the Treasure

Any treasure, before it is sought, appreciated, prized, and protected, must first be recognized as a real treasure. This applies to Jesus more than to anything or anyone else. He is the treasure of treasures!

I want to tell you another little story, hoping that you believe me this time more quickly than when I wrote about giving away those millions. Several years

Jesus Christ is the indisputable treasure of treasures, our God of Creation, worth more than anything and everything he ever created.

ago, a man went into one of those nature stores—not a jewelry store selling precious gems but the kind of place found in many malls today, where rocks, minerals, fossils, butterflies, and floral specimens from the world of nature are on display. On the store shelves were beautiful mineral specimens of every shape, size, and color: onyx and quartz, geodes and crystals. This man didn't glance at any of these. He bent down to examine a box of dirty rocks on the floor, not too far from the cash register. His hands were soon blackened with dust and grime, but he eventually lifted a specimen from the box that interested him greatly. He took it to the shop owner, asking if it were for sale. The owner took a casual glance and answered, "Sure!" The man then wanted to know, "How much are you asking?" After another quick glance the owner responded even more casually, "Two-fifty." The customer with the dusty knees and dirty hands gave him $2.50, and walked out of the store, taking with him the largest ruby ever discovered in the history of our planet.

As reported in magazines and on TV, one year after he bought that ruby for two dollars and fifty cents, the man sold it for two-and-one-half million dollars, exactly one million times more than he paid. Two people held the treasure in their hands, the owner of the shop and the man who dug it out of the box. Only one of the two recognized the treasure, and he is the one who became the millionaire.

Jesus Christ is the indisputable treasure of treasures, our God of Creation, worth more than anything and everything he ever created. Before we can successfully make him known to others, we ourselves must first recognize him as the most valuable treasure of all. Evangelizers do not climb to the housetops to expound dry concepts. We can collect all the dry concepts we want by taking an extended course in the history of philosophy. Who is ready to live by or to die for a bunch of dry concepts? Nobody! Evangelizers go to the housetops to shout out the name of a living and loving Savior whom they know personally and are very anxious to introduce to others.

The Best News Ever Carried

A favorite weekly program in the early years of television was called *The Millionaire*. In the opening scenes of each episode, a gentleman was shown writing at his desk. You never saw the man's face—only his arm and the impressive desktop as he sat filling out a bank check. First he wrote the date, and then the name of a person or family or some good work, such as an orphanage, hospital, research laboratory, or center for social services. Then he carefully wrote in the amount of the check: one million dollars. Finally, he signed the check and gave it to the dignified lawyer standing at his side. After handing over the check, the philanthropist explained why this time he was giving his latest million-dollar donation to this particular person or project.

The lawyer then had the check bank certified, meaning that the million dollars was locked into the bank account until this particular check was brought in for deposit. In other words, once certified, the bank check was as good as cash in the hands of the one to whom it was written.

We then saw the lawyer knocking on the door of the unsuspecting beneficiary of the incredible gift. When the door opened, the lawyer gave that person the surprising news. "I have here—for you—a bank-certified check of one million dollars." As it developed, the story of that week's show told what happened to the person or family or good work, when, suddenly and out of the blue, a donation of one million dollars came their way.

Now imagine for a moment that you got the knock at your door. You opened—not to the news that someone was bringing you a gift of only a million dollars, but to the more astounding news that here for you was the gift of an absolutely incredible, unimaginable, and inexpressible fortune going far beyond your wildest hopes and dreams. Then, after showing you the magnitude of that fortune, the person knocking at your door added something that the fictional lawyer in the television show never said: "But I must explain that the person who sent me to you with this wondrous and vast fortune first had to do something very difficult in order to enrich you in this way. That person first had to die for you!"

What would you do after receiving that kind of news? Would you just mouth a quick "thank you" and calmly close the door? I don't think so. I think you would be overcome with curiosity. Making sure the messenger didn't slip away, wouldn't you say, "Please come in and sit down. Let me get you some coffee. We have to talk. There are things I have to ask, things I need to know about the person who sent you to me with this startling good news. What was his name and exactly who was he? Where did he come from, and when and in what way did he give his life for me? And most importantly, please tell me *why* he did it for *me*."

You already had that kind of a knock on your own door. Perhaps, as with so many of us, it was your own parents who, in your early childhood, were the first to share with you such an astonishing piece of good news.

But now you are the one being sent by God, Master of the Countless Millions, to carry this piece of great Good News from door to door. This means you must have the answers to these questions at the very tip of *your* tongue. You can't do your job well unless you are capable of satisfying and answering all the curiosity that this very best piece of Good News instills in all who hear it.

Answering the Important Questions

Let's take a look at the questions, and spend a little time studying and praying about the answers.

1. What is the name of our incomparable benefactor? Hunting carefully through the pages of Scripture, how many different names and titles do you find referring to Jesus? Certainly more than one or two, or even five or ten! To the question of why our Lord is given so many names, the answer is easy. Jesus Christ is so wonderfully good, so amazingly loving and merciful, so divinely powerful and wise, that there is no one name or even a small package of names that can fully express all of his greatness and grandeur. We need a whole long list of names and titles, each of them revealing a bit more of his infinite goodness and wonder.

So, of course he is called the *Christ*, the *Anointed*, the *Holy One of God*. When Isaiah prophesies his coming, he is so overcome with amazement that he starts right off by giving Jesus no less than four different names (Isaiah 9:6). Isaiah calls him a *Wonder-Counselor*, and that saves us a lot of money spent on visits to psychiatrists and the purchase of expensive sedatives. He calls the Messiah our *God-Hero*, and what a hero he is. Superman, favorite hero of our fantasies, stretches out his arms to catch up Lois Lane tumbling from a helicopter and carries her to safety. Jesus Christ stretches out his arms on the cross to catch up all of humanity and carries us safely to salvation and eternal life. What a hero! The third name Isaiah gives our Lord is *Father Forever,* pointing to Jesus as the one person capable of revealing the Father to us as Abba, our Daddy God of Love. Finally, Isaiah calls Jesus *Prince of Peace*, and if we already possessed all the glittering pleasures, power, and wealth of the world but lacked the peace that only Christ can give, we would have absolutely nothing. We would be so destitute that we might start looking for escape in alcohol, drugs, or even a desperate bullet.

We read in other scriptural passages that Jesus is the promised *Messiah*, our *Savior*, the one and only *Redeemer* of all mankind. I particularly appreciate that last title. The motto of my own Redemptorist community is the text, "With him is abundant redemption" (Psalm 130:7). As Redeemer, Jesus willingly pays whatever ransom is demanded in order to set us free. If the ransom Jesus must pay is five dollars or five million or five billion dollars, he pays it without a moment's hesitation. Years ago, before entering the seminary, a fellow Redemptorist was studying at Miami University, preparing for a business career. His name was Raphael, and one day in prayer he heard Jesus speak these words to him: "Rafi, if it were necessary, tomorrow I would go again to Calvary to die a second time just for you." When Raphael heard those words, he was so touched by the depth of Christ's love that he immediately packed up and left the university to enter the Redemptorist seminary.

The Bible also refers to our Lord as the *Word of Eternal Life*. His most sublime title is *Son of God*, but he is also *Son of Man*, *Son of Mary*, *Son of David*, *Son of Jacob*, and *Root of Jesse*. He is the *Light of Life*, our *Morning Star*, and if that star isn't there to enlighten our day, we walk in darkness. Jesus is the *King of Glory*, the *King of Kings*, the *Lord of Lords*, the *Light* that has come into the world. He is

He is the *Light of Life*, our *Morning Star*, and if that star isn't there to enlighten our day, we walk in darkness.

Emmanuel, our *God with Us* who promises never to leave us. He is *Jesus*, the living proclamation that Yahweh is our salvation. He is our *Way*, and there is no other; the *Truth* that sets us free; the *Life* that leads us to a paradise lasting forever. He alone is our *Alpha* and *Omega*, the beginning and end of everything we are and do and hope to be.

"There is no other name under heaven given among men by which we must be saved" (Acts 4:12). His is "the name which is above every name," and at that name, "every knee should bow, in heaven and on earth and under the earth, and every tongue confess that Jesus Christ is Lord" (Philippians 2:9-11)!

2. Who is he? Thomas the Apostle shouted out the answer when he fell to his knees and cried out, "My Lord and my God!" (John 20:28). God sent Moses with these instructions: "Thus you shall say to the Israelites, 'I AM has sent me to you' " (Exodus 3:14). Three times in the eighth chapter of John's Gospel, we hear Jesus calling himself, "I AM" (John 8:24,28,58, NAB). He is saying, "It is I who have no yesterday and will have no tomorrow. To me nothing can be added, and nothing taken away. I am eternal, and infinite. I am your God and there is no other, no one equal or comparable to me."

He is the one who is both God and man, and therefore the only person who can save us. As Son of God, he is divine and therefore capable of paying our infinite ransom. As Son of Mary, he is human and therefore capable of making that payment for us and as one of us! He is the love of God made visible so that we can look upon him and see that God is love (1 John 4:8). He is the spotless slaughtered Lamb, the Good Shepherd, our friend and brother, our Lord, God, and King. Pope John Paul II instructed us to seek "a renewed appreciation" of "who Christ truly is," in that way coming to know him as "the one Mediator between God and man and the sole Redeemer of the world" (*Tertio Millennio Adveniente*, 40, 38).

3. Where did Jesus come from? We can never answer this question with the name of a place, not even the place called heaven. We believe that Jesus Christ is God himself, and God does not fit in a place. All places have limits, but God is limitless, borderless! John the Apostle is mystical and poetic in answering the question of where Jesus came from, with words that all Christians seem to know by heart: "In the beginning was the Word, and the Word was with God, and the Word was God. . . . And the Word became flesh, and dwelt among us" (John 1:1,14). Jesus, one in being with the Father, comes to us from the Father so that he can become our sure way back to the Father.

4. How and when did he come? Where did he live and die? If Jesus came from God, what is the date of his coming, and in what town was he born? Where did he live, and under what circumstances did he die? We are the reporters of this magnificent story, and newspaper editors send their reporter out to cover a story with the instructions, "Get the facts!" The story of Jesus is a love story like no other, and this story is fact rather than fiction. The love stories we call *romances* are often told in the context of a passion of pleasure. This story is proven true by being told in the context of a passion of pain, the passion and death of Jesus on the cross.

No one can tell the story well by dryly reading from the pages of a book. No, we must first write the story of this innocent Lamb who shed his blood for us on our hearts. Then, by reading it from our hearts, we can set other hearts on fire with love.

5. Why did Jesus die for me? He had two reasons; both were impelling. He needed only one!

First of all, Jesus went to the cross and bled to death for us because his heavenly Father sent him to do so. "My food is to do the will of him who *sent* me and to complete his work" (John 4:34). If the Father willed that he be executed in the most painful way ever imagined, well that was fine with him. "Father . . . not what I want but what you want. . . . Your will be done" (Matthew 26:39,42).

The second reason Jesus died for us was simpler and even more incredible. He loves us so much that he is more than ready to die, so that "in him we might become the righteousness of God" (2 Corinthians 5:21). "Christ loved us and handed himself over for us as a sacrificial offering to God" (Ephesians 5:2, NAB). When he spoke those endearing words, "No one has greater love than this, to lay down one's life for one's friends; you are my friends" (John 15:13-14), Jesus was telling us exactly what motivated him to die for us.

The Greatest Love Story

Let's take this last thought and try to capture its relevance to our modern world. Imagine that an attractive young woman in today's fast-moving culture lives in Los Angeles and has an opportunity to meet some famous movie star named Leonardo So-and-So or Tom Whatever. They have a few dates and dinners together, spending time getting to know each other. Then one day the phone rings, and when she picks it up, the young woman recognizes the famous voice of that handsome movie star about whom all the other girls are dreaming. It's Leonardo What's-His-Name or Whoever, and he says to her the words the other girls all yearn to hear: "I am calling to tell you that I love you and want to give myself totally to you." He of course says all this better than you or I could ever say it. He's the movie star, trained and paid well to say things just like that. When the girl hears these romantic words, what does she do? I'll tell you what she does! She doesn't put the phone down for forty-eight hours. She calls all of her relatives and friends, everyone she knows and doesn't know, and everyone whose name she finds in the telephone book, giving them her sensational bit of good news: "Leonardo, the handsome, famous, and desirable movie star, loves ME!"

That isn't really the greatest piece of news that the world has ever heard. The big news, the best news ever communicated, is the astonishing revealed truth that we have all gotten exactly that "phone call" from God himself. The Creator of the earth, the Savior of the world, loves us so much that he has given his life for us on a blood-soaked cross. If that young woman rushes to spread the news of a film star confessing his love for her, imagine how excited and active each of us should be with the news of a divine love transforming us into the very Bride of Christ.

Walking down the aisle of a bookstore, you can suddenly come across whole shelves of books with frilly pink covers. Above them, you see a sign reading, *Romances!* Romantic novels touch hearts and stir emotions because they tell tales of a love so great that it impels the hero to cross the desert, swim a river, climb to a mountaintop, sail an ocean, and pass through great barriers of pain to reach the woman he loves. As Christians, we don't need to read about the adventures of *Doctor Zhivago* or any of the other stories to get goose pimples or feel the thrill. We are touched to the heart by the greatest romance of all, the story of our God in flesh, traveling from heaven to the hill of Calvary to make known the immensity and passion of his love for us. To write that story on the hearts of others in ways that transform their lives, we must first have our own hearts transfixed by the story and the truth of this greatest of all love stories.

The Key to Becoming an Effective Evangelizer

The story of Andrew the Apostle that we read in the first chapter of John's Gospel points to the spiritual experience that transforms each of us into capable evangelizers. Andrew was originally a disciple of John the Baptist. John was given the mission of leading others to Christ, so he sends Andrew and a companion off to search out this Jesus of Nazareth about whom everyone is talking. Following the crowds, Andrew comes upon our Lord and by a grace from the Holy Spirit, quickly recognizes him to be the long-awaited Messiah. We read that immediately after this moment of recognition, Andrew, together with his companion, "came and saw where [Jesus] was staying, and they remained with him that day" (John 1:39). This means that Andrew followed our Lord through the street, never taking his eyes off him. He studied how he greeted and helped the sick and the poor, how he attended the little children, and how he had a word, a smile, and an expression of love for everyone he passed.

Andrew spent the rest of that day with our Lord, looking into his eyes to capture the tenderness, hearing his words, and being thrilled by his wisdom—sensing all of the qualities and strengths that are found in no one else, not even the great Baptist himself. In other words, Andrew set aside every moment he could for the sole purpose of getting to know the wondrous personality of Jesus of Nazareth.

The very next words lay out the key to becoming zealous and confident evangelizers. "[Andrew] *first* found his brother Simon and said to him, 'We have found the Messiah'" (John 1:41; italics added). Now try to imagine exactly how Andrew spoke those words. For centuries and even millenniums, every Israelite dreamed of having that piece of good news to carry, and now Andrew was the one crying it out with a joy and excitement that almost lifted him off the ground. The next words we read are these: "[Andrew] brought Simon to Jesus" (John 1:42). That is exactly how Simon the Fisherman became Peter the Apostle.

In a nutshell, those few verses of John's Gospel tell us that to become an evangelizer, we must first make a serious effort to seek out Jesus and spend generous amounts of time getting to know him. Impelled by the excitement and blessings of having discovered and recognized the world's only Savior, we will almost automatically set off to tell others about the Messiah we now know, bringing as many as we can to meet, recognize, love, and follow him along the pathway to holiness.

It's that simple! To evangelize with power we must be ready to say with St. Paul, "I count everything as loss because of the surpassing worth of knowing Christ Jesus my Lord. For his sake I have suffered the loss of all things, and count them as refuse . . . that I may know him and the power of his resurrection" (Philippians 3:8,10).

Evangelization is an effort to illuminate human hearts with the light of Christ. How can we do that if we do not walk in that light ourselves? "Whoever follows me will never walk in darkness but will have the light of life" (John 8:12). To evangelize means that we must paint for others a beautiful portrait of Christ that attracts them to him. How can we do that successfully if we ourselves have never sought and come to know the face of Christ? (*Novo Millennio Ineunte*, 16-28). Evangelizers shout out the Good News for all to hear! What can motivate them to do it if they have never "tasted that the Lord is good?" (1 Peter 2:3). Evangelization is the task of proclaiming the victorious Christ who is alive and with us today. How do I do that if I have never met the risen Lord?

Getting to Know Jesus

Jesus promises to make himself known to us with these words: "The sheep follow him because they know his voice. . . . I am the good shepherd. I know my own and my own know me" (John 10:4,14). In very practical terms, exactly what can we do in order to come to know Jesus personally?

Evangelization is an effort to illuminate human hearts with the light of Christ.

1. Put time and effort into proclaiming your love for Christ. I especially enjoy and appreciate this first way of coming to know Christ personally, because it is so clear and simple. Why don't you actually do it as you go along reading these instructions? Say in your heart, or even out loud in a clear voice, "Jesus, I love you." Now, say it again: "I love you, I love you, love you, love you, love you. I really love you, dearest Jesus." That's it, that's all there is to it! And it really works, because Jesus has made us the promise: "Those who love me will be loved by my Father, and I will love them *and reveal myself to them*" (John 14:21; italics added). Make the noise. Proclaim your own love for Christ. Let others hear you saying that you love him, and Jesus must keep his promise to reveal himself to you. Isn't he always faithful to his promises (Psalm 145:13)?

2. Talk prayerfully with our Lord. The normal way friends get to know each other is by spending time talking together.

Time spent talking with God is called *prayer*, and our prayers should be real conversations. This means that at least two people should have a chance to speak, and this leads us to a practical piece of advice: "When you pray, don't forget to shut up and listen!" We read in the Bible how "the LORD used to speak to Moses face to face, as one speaks to a friend" (Exodus 33:11). Moses, though, is not God's only friend. Doesn't Jesus say to all of us, "You are my friends" (John 15:14)? This means that in our prayers we can expect to hear from him, and by listening to him carefully, we will be getting to know him better and better.

I wouldn't be too impressed if someone said to me, "I know Tom Cruise; I've seen all of his films." It would be more impressive to hear a person say, "I know Tom Cruise, the movie star. We have lunch and talk together several times each week." In the same way, it is not that impressive to hear someone saying, "I know Jesus of Nazareth; I saw the movie eighteen times." Much more convincing is to hear him saying, "I know Jesus Christ very personally. We talk together in prayer every single day."

This thought applies not only to prayers of meditation and contemplation but to prayers of petition as well. The scriptural promise in this regard is this: "You shall call, and the LORD will answer; you shall cry for help, and he will say, Here I am" (Isaiah 58:9). Whenever we experience our Lord being here for us, whenever he fulfills his promise to answer our prayers, he is revealing to us his goodness and concern for us, his nearness to us, the intensity of his love, his fidelity, and his infinite power. I believe that Jesus tells us again and again to ask, to seek, and to knock, simply because he is so anxious to reveal himself by opening to us the door to his heart.

3. Meet Jesus in the sacraments. I could pick any of the seven sacraments to exemplify this point, but let's just take that glorious sacrament of mercy and reconciliation that we call Confession. No one is going to say that listing for someone else our failures and sins is a favorite activity. Yet whenever we do so, Jesus takes advantage of this opportunity by revealing to us his mercy and patience, his healing power and his gentleness, his quickness to forgive, and his love for us that so easily weather any and all of our sins.

I remember once giving a retreat at a home for troubled girls. One of the young women made a confession for the very first time in her life. The good sisters helping the girls told me afterwards that when she came from the confessional, the girl ran through the dining room of the school, jumping over all the chairs and even the tables.

We define sacraments as signs instituted by Christ for giving grace, and those signs send very clear signals—few of them more loudly than the Sacrament of Reconciliation. Someone entering the confessional feels the weight of his or her sins and shortcomings. They come from the sacrament actually and almost physically feeling that the weight of sin and guilt has been lifted from them and that they have been made new and free.

It may not be easy to go to confession, but it is delightful to return from it, liberated by a convincing sign declaring that all our sins have disappeared, and encouraged by the depths of mercy, patience, and forgiveness that God has shown us.

4. Spend some quality time with your heavenly friend.

Doing this is what we call "making a retreat." Jesus invites us to such an experience with the same words he once spoke to his apostles: " 'Come away to a deserted place all by yourselves and rest a while.'. . . And they went away in the boat to a deserted place by themselves" (Mark 6:31-32). When two people go off for a bit of vacation together, they are heading for one of their best opportunities to get to know and enjoy each other. A retreat is exactly that, a vacation with Jesus Christ, a very nice time together with a very nice person!

5. Listen carefully to those who know Jesus well.

People are anxious to hear about famous personalities that others have met. Saints are the lucky ones who, more successfully than the rest of us, have gotten to know Jesus exceptionally well. By carefully reading the mystical works of Teresa of Avila or enjoying the exquisite autobiography of Thérèse of Lisieux or by pondering the simple yet rich words of Mother Teresa of Calcutta, we have an opportunity to capture something of what these saints learned during their lifetimes about the personality, words, and works of our Lord and

Savior, Jesus Christ. Saints, together with St. Paul, can honestly say, "It is Christ who lives in me" (Galatians 2:20). Mother Teresa constantly told her sisters that anyone who meets them should be meeting Christ in them. All of the saints are a revelation of the heart and mind of Christ, and therefore they are people well worth listening to.

6. Walk in the footsteps of the Good Shepherd. There is only one person who can say that he or she knows the Good Shepherd, and that is the person who walks in his footsteps, following him wherever he leads. Jesus told us that his sheep know and follow behind him, because they recognize his voice (John 10:4,14). No one finds out where the Good Shepherd takes him or her simply by reading Psalm 23. Only by allowing him to lead them do they reach the green pastures, drink of the crystal clear water, find themselves seated at the banquet table, and have their feet solidly planted on the path of righteousness, their heads anointed with the oil of royalty. Only those persons who walk humbly and obediently in the footsteps of Christ can cry out joyfully, "The Lord is my shepherd, I shall not want. . . . My cup overflows. . . . Surely goodness and mercy shall follow me all the days of my life" (Psalm 23:1,5-6).

St. James tells us that if we draw near to God, he in turn will draw near to us (James 4:8). And Christ's own promise is this: "Those who love me will keep my word, and my Father will love them, and we will come to them and make our home with them" (John 14:23). Those who share the same dwelling certainly get to know each other very well, and that is exactly what we share with Jesus once we start living his word.

7. Meet Jesus in the breaking of the bread. The best way of all to meet Christ is eucharistically. The Eucharist is a spiritual act of marital love between Jesus and his beloved Bride, the Church. As members of the Church, each of us can experience the intimacy of becoming one body with our heavenly Spouse. Those two disciples walking along despairingly on the road to Emmaus failed to realize that they were walking with their victorious Savior. As they told the story to the Apostles after returning to Jerusalem, their hearts were burning within them, but they only came to know him "in the breaking of the bread" (Luke 24:35).

It is so easy for us to walk up to Holy Communion thinking only of what we are planning for dinner or to return to our benches from the altar rail distracted with hopes of seeing our team winning the big ball game. By very deliberately focusing on the truth that Jesus walks with us on our own daily road to Emmaus, we too can experience a revelation of his presence and personality in the breaking of the bread. "Be still, and know that I am God" (Psalm 46:10).

An Evangelizer's Ultimate Qualification

Traveling around the world, I have mentioned on different occasions that I met Pope John Paul II and knew dear

Mother Teresa very well. I spoke with the Pope on a number of different occasions, having breakfast, lunch, and dinner meetings with him eight different times. I cannot give the exact number of times that I spoke and worked with Mother Teresa—probably fifty or more. People can be very impressed to hear that I ate with a pope and spoke with a saint. This means that I had opportunities for getting to know them personally, but that does not qualify me as an evangelizer. I am an evangelizer only if I can say that I have met and have gotten to know Jesus, the Savior whom we have been sent to proclaim.

It was delightful and thrilling to meet the pope and the saint, but we all have to do better than that. Our challenge is to speak with others about a Jesus whom we have met and know personally, and with whom we are now coworkers in the vineyard of the Lord (1 Corinthians 3:9). Knowing Jesus allows us to speak about him as a friend, the best friend we could possible have; a friend so good, so loving, so kind and powerful, so delightful and charming and important that we yearn to introduce him to everyone we can. I've had the joy of introducing friends, relatives, and coworkers to both the pope and Mother Teresa, and I never did it without experiencing great joy.

Having a friend like that is such Good News that we have to shout it from the housetops: I know Jesus Christ! Come and meet the Messiah I have found, the Savior, the Brother, the Friend, the Teacher, the Shepherd, the Master, the Lord, the King, and God that I know and follow and love with all of my heart and would really enjoy introducing to you. Introducing others to Christ is the joy of joys. Doing so is the very definition of evangelization. ⊓

Chapter 5

Prayer: The Tool in Everyone's Hands

Blessed John XXIII invited us to "perfume all of our actions with the life-giving breath of prayer." Pope John Paul II applies this important piece of good advice to the task of evangelization: "Among the forms of sharing, first place goes to spiritual cooperation through prayer. . . . Prayer should accompany the journey of missionaries so that the proclamation of the word will be effective through God's grace" (*Redemptoris Missio*, 78).

Why does Pope John Paul give prayer nothing less than top priority? For the simple reason that any success in spreading the Good News requires faith, and faith comes only as a free gift from God! Listen to two other quotes from *Redemptoris Missio* that spell this out: "The Church serves the Kingdom by her intercession, since the Kingdom by its very nature is God's gift and work. . . . The mission of the Church, like that of Jesus, is God's work or, as Luke often puts it, the work of the Spirit" (20,24).

Tertullian, an ancient Christian apologist and writer, saw prayer as "the only thing that can conquer God." It is the one action of ours that makes God's power accessible, and since our mission calls for nothing less than divine power, the clear and easy conclusion is that we must pray—and pray hard. Again in the pope's own words, "Mission, then, is based not on human abilities but on the power of the risen Lord" (*Redemptoris Missio*, 23).

Both Paul VI and John Paul II echoed this thought when they refer to the Holy Spirit as "the principal agent of evangelization" (*Evangelii Nuntiandi*, 75; *Redemptoris Missio*, 21). As God's power personified, the

Holy Spirit makes it all happen, and we never spend our time more wisely than when we are begging him to do just that. Coming as the fruit of those prayers, nothing can be more delightful than to see the Holy Spirit using us, weak as we are, to spread his blessings and graces around the world.

This is no new thought in the Catholic Church. Way back in my seminary days (over fifty years ago), I remember hearing this little story about the key to effective preaching. It seems that a famous preacher of parish missions grew far too impressed with his own success. When he began to do a bit of bragging from the pulpit, God decided to set him straight. He sent an angel in a dream to explain to the proud preacher that his own words and brilliant thoughts were not bringing about all the conversions

We must stockpile God's graces. Prayer alone wins us those graces.

and impressive confessions. These great fruits were flowing from the intercessory prayers of the humble lay brother traveling with him. Hidden on a little bench at the foot of the pulpit, the brother was praying his heart out, begging God to add divine grace to the preacher's lofty words. Those graces, rather than the sounds ringing out from the pulpit, were what were changing people's hearts and lives.

How could this understanding of evangelization and our role in it be more thrilling? God himself is accomplishing the great work of salvation, and because the task is so demanding and difficult, the Father sent his only Son to do the job at a terrible cost: "He . . . did not spare his own Son, but gave him up for the sake of all of us" (Romans 8:32). The Son then gave us a share in the mission, and because it is so humanly impossible, he repeatedly instructs us to pray. "Truly, truly, I say to you, he who believes in me will also do the works that I do; and greater works than these will he do; . . . Whatever you ask in my name, I will do it, that the Father may be glorified in the Son; if you ask anything in my name, I will do it" (John 14:12-14).

The mission is harder than walking on water—more like bringing us back to life through a resurrection from the death of sin. It is more difficult than multiplying loaves and fishes—more like calming the storms of all our dominating passions and human emotions! It is far more complicated than healing the sick—more like leading people to a transforming rebirth through the blood of the Lamb and the waters of baptism!

It is the biggest, best, hardest, and most necessary task anyone has ever been called upon to accomplish! And that's why we must pray, while inviting everyone else to join with us in lifting up those prayers. Nations stockpile bullets, bombs, and missiles for war, but because our battle is "against the authorities, against the cosmic powers of this present darkness, against the spiritual forces of evil in the heavenly places" (Ephesians 6:12), we must stockpile God's graces. Prayer alone wins us those graces!

If we ever succeeded in getting a whole parish, or better still the whole Church, to join together in prayer, wonderful and even miraculous things would begin to happen. Let me tell a personal story about how powerful the prayers of a whole parish can be. At a time when I was pastor in a coastal town of Puerto Rico, there was a seven-year-old boy in the parish who had completely lost sight in one eye. When he began to experience trouble with his other eye, the mother brought him to the doctor, who examined him and declared a state of emergency, telling the boy's mom that if an operation were not performed as soon as possible, the child would quickly lose sight in his good eye and remain totally blind. The operation took place,

How many realize that intercessory prayer brings us to a high level of adoration?

with the entire parish praying intently for its success.

A few days later, the doctor visited the boy, whose good eye was now heavily bandaged. When she walked into the hospital room to see her patient, the boy saw her—with his blind eye. After the bandage was removed from the other eye, he was seeing well with both eyes.

The doctor related what had happened to another surgeon, reputed to be the best eye specialist in all of Puerto Rico, asking him to come and examine the boy. The brilliant surgeon refused to do so, declaring angrily, "Such a thing is not possible!" I suspect that the doctor was afraid to find out, not only that it was possible, but also that there was a more brilliant Heavenly Eye Doctor busy at work in the same hospital.

What would happen if the whole Church, with its hundreds of millions of members, suddenly became a spiritual powerhouse of prayer, begging God to keep busy giving surprising and even miraculous successes to all of our evangelistic operations? I heard a speaker once define our biggest problem to be "the sad fact that the Church today is more of a 'Martha' than a 'Mary.' " We often hear people being congratulated with these words: "You did a great job!" How many, though, are told: "You are a great person of prayer"? How many realize that intercessory prayer brings us to a high level of adoration, placing us as it does in just the right position before God—as weak and dependent creatures standing humbly before the greatness of our generous and all-powerful Creator?

Mountain Movers

Here are a few examples of some very effective people in the history of the Church, who knew well that God's work is accomplished only with the indispensable help and grace of God, a grace only tapped through prayer. The great mountain movers of history are people who prayed, and who obviously prayed very hard.

MOSES: How did he win battles? "Moses' hands grew weary; so they took a stone and put it under him, and he sat upon it, and Aaron and Hur held up his hands, one on one side, and the other on the other side; so his hands were steady until the going down of the sun. And Joshua mowed down Amalek and his people with the edge of the sword" (Exodus 17:12-13). How did Moses gain God's patience for the Israelites? "Pardon the iniquity of this people, I pray thee, according to the greatness of thy steadfast love, and according as thou hast forgiven this people, from Egypt even until now. Then the LORD said, 'I have pardoned, according to your word'" (Numbers 14:19-20). How did Moses save the Israelites and his brother Aaron from God's wrath? "I was afraid of the anger and hot displeasure which the

> **Mother Teresa loved to talk— not about what was she was doing but about the things she saw Jesus doing around her.**

LORD bore against you, so that he was ready to destroy you. But the LORD hearkened to me that time also. The LORD was so angry with Aaron that he was ready to destroy him; and I prayed for Aaron also at the same time" (Deuteronomy 9:20).

ST. MONICA: She prayed thirty-two years for her son. A bishop finally told her: "Go now, I beg you; it is not possible that the son of so many tears should perish." Not her words but her prayers did the job, and Augustine, her scandalous son, was converted into one of the greatest saints the Church has ever known. Monica died at the age of fifty-five, just nine days after Augustine was baptized. This means that she started praying for his conversion when still a young twenty-three-year-old mother.

MOTHER TERESA: She loved to talk—not about what was she was doing but about the things she saw Jesus doing around her. Others asked her prayers, but she was always quick to seek their prayers with these words: "Pray for me, that I do not damage the work of God." Her regular prayer request to priests was: "When you pour the drops of water into the chalice at Mass, please ask Jesus to make me that little drop of water mixed with his Blood."

POPE JOHN PAUL II: In *Redemptoris Missio*, the pope writes that "the missionary must be a 'contemplative in action.' . . . Unless the missionary is a contemplative, he cannot proclaim Christ in a credible way" (91). This pope, described by *Time* magazine as "rarely off his knees" and by *Newsweek* as spending up to six hours a day in prayer, reminds us to utilize the pains and sacrifices of the sick and infirm in our own prayer campaigns: "I therefore urge those engaged in the pastoral care of the sick to teach them about the efficacy of suffering, and to encourage them to offer their sufferings to God for missionaries. By making such an offering, the sick themselves become missionaries" (78).

OUR BLESSED MOTHER: She prayed the best of all prayers: "Do with me what you want!" (see Luke 1:38). Through the centuries, she keeps coming back from heaven just to ask our prayers, leading Pope John Paul II to proclaim Mary as our "model of that maternal love which should inspire all who cooperate in the Church's apostolic mission" (*Redemptoris Missio*, 92).

Spiritual Sit-Down Strikes

Years ago, we read in newspapers about people going on *sit-down strikes*! Well, we have to be God's sit-down/kneel-down people, with no intention of moving until our prayers obtain what is so badly needed in the Church today: a new enthusiasm and power for working dynamically and successfully at the task of evangelizing the whole world. Listen to the language Jesus himself uses in urging us to undertake our own "sit-down strike" of prayer: "Which of you, desiring to build a tower, does not *first sit down* and count the cost, whether he has enough to complete it? . . . Or what king, going to encounter another king in war, will not *sit down first* and take counsel whether he is able with ten thousand to meet him who comes against him with twenty thousand?" (Luke 14:28,31; italics added).

What wise and humble evangelizer will not sit down first in order to talk over with God the challenges of the task ahead, confident that no matter how powerful the enemy, God will see to it that we end up on the winning side? We clearly need more "Marys" in the Church, working hand-in-hand with all the "Marthas," to guarantee that we have everything needed for doing the job and doing it well!

All of us together must storm heaven just the way the people of Judah did centuries ago:

> Judah assembled to seek help from the LORD; from all the cities of Judah they came to seek the LORD. . . . All the men of Judah stood before the LORD, with their little ones, their wives, and their children. . . . All Judah and the inhabitants

of Jerusalem fell down before the LORD, wor-
shiping the LORD. And the Levites, of the
Kohathites and the Korahites, stood up to praise
the LORD, the God of Israel, with a very loud
voice. . . . [Jehoshaphat] appointed those who were
to sing to the LORD and praise him in holy array,
as they went before the army . . . And when they
began to sing and praise, the LORD set an ambush
against the men of Ammon, Moab, and Mount
Seir, who had come against Judah, so that they
were routed. . . . They came to Jerusalem, with
harps and lyres and trumpets, to the house of the
LORD. (2 Chronicles 20:4-28)

Of course Judah won that battle! And we too can
win the world for Christ if we keep praying *together* with
that same kind of intensity. "Let us then with confidence draw near to the throne of grace, that we may
receive mercy and find grace to help in time of need"
(Hebrews 4:16). "The LORD has heard my supplication;
the LORD accepts my prayer" (Psalm 6:9).

Trying to do the job without prayer would make us
seem about as arrogant as that old TV commercial
where the announcer kept crying out so confidently,
"We do everything possible to satisfy our customers; the
impossible just takes us a little longer!" No! The impossible takes longer time at prayer! The impossible takes a
determined and prayerful dependence upon God, for
whom alone all things are possible.

I want to add the beautiful concluding words of *Redemptoris Missio:* "To 'Mary's mediation, wholly oriented towards Christ and tending to the revelation of his salvific power,' I entrust the Church and, in particular, those who commit themselves to carrying out the MISSIONARY MANDATE in today's world" (92; emphasis added).

Evangelization truly is the universal mission of the Church. With your voice, and not without your prayers, we can all be an important part of that mission and a vital factor in bringing about its success from one end of the earth to the other! ⊓

Chapter 6

Go with Urgency!

Four words sum up and define the whole of Christian life:

1."COME!" Recognize me as the Christ, your only Savior in whom you can place all of your faith and hopes, and from whom you must learn to love!

2."FOLLOW ME!" Stay with me; live with me and for me! Learn from me, and come to know me as the way, the truth and the life, your indispensable wisdom from above!

3."RECEIVE!" I have promised you life in abundance together with the full power of my Holy Spirit. Open yourself to these great gifts.

4."GO!" I have an important job for you! I commission you and send you forth, expecting you to work hard to produce fruit in abundance, fruit that will last!

After giving so many talks about that fourth word which impels us to *get going*, I've gotten a bit nervous about the possibility of being labeled a "go-go" priest! Not really that frightened, though, because a title like that would actually put me in some pretty good company.

The word "go" is used 1,514 times in the Bible, 233 times in the New Testament, 54 times in Matthew's Gospel alone. Jesus said *go* and be reconciled; *go* two miles with anyone asking you to go a mile; *go* to the other side of the lake; *go* seeking out my lost sheep; *go* and tell John; *go* and sell all you have and invite all whom you meet. And finally he commissions us to go with these decisive words: "Go on your way. See, I am sending you out like lambs into the midst of wolves" (Luke 10:3). "Go therefore and make disciples of all nations" (Matthew 28:19).

This mission of calling all Christians to get moving at the task of carrying the Good News to the ends of the earth is like the job of space engineers, who push buttons that launch a rocket on its way to the moon. Actually, we need even more force and power than that. More than sending a spaceship to Jupiter or the moon, we are trying to get a majority of mankind all the way to God, all the way to heavenly glory! That's going to take a lot more thrust!

The first push in that direction came on Pentecost Sunday two thousand years ago. Five minutes after his arrival, the Holy Spirit had the Apostles out on the streets of Jerusalem and heading off to Spain and India and everywhere else to evangelize with a courage that ultimately cost them their lives.

I have a natural inclination to grow impatient when I see something requiring dynamic action or an immediate response being left undone, or being done slowly and too late to make a difference! This kind of reaction hits me even at the movies: "Sir, there are unidentified planes heading for Pearl Harbor" . . . "Oh, probably just another false alarm!" "Officer, someone's trying to kill me" . . . "Okay lady, but don't get too excited; First I need your social security number." "Sergeant, don't let anyone in this room!" . . . "No trouble, Captain, but first I'll just slip outside for a quick smoke."

For me, the reverse is also true. It is pure excitement and greatly appreciated to see an emergency or some threatening need met with dynamic and immediate action. An example from the movies is that very old adventure film, *Tarzan Finds a Son*. The little fellow called "Boy" is caught in a giant spider web, and lets out his boyish Tarzan yodel. Tarzan yodels back as only Tarzan can, and then he starts to run faster than a rhinoceros, overtaking a herd of antelopes, swinging through trees more swiftly than the apes! He knew that the situation was urgent and that no time could be wasted. So he responded immediately and dynamically, and of course arrived just in the nick of time.

To a far greater degree, Jesus saw his own mission as extremely urgent. Even as a small boy, he explained: "I must be about my father's business" (Luke 2:49, KJV). In handing on his mission to us, the language he uses again has urgency: "Go out *at once* into the streets and lanes of the town and bring in the poor, the crippled, the blind, and the lame" (Luke 14:21, italics added). An angel's words are equally urgent when he commands the women at the tomb to "Go *quickly* and tell his disciples, 'He has been raised from the dead.' " This very determined angel seemed to be saying: "Now, no hesitation or excuses; get going and fast!"

The women seemed to hear the angelic message clearly, for the next words we read are, "So they left the tomb *quickly* with fear and great joy, and ran to tell his disciples" (Matthew 28:7-8, italics added).

After the ascension, instructions from another angel were equally urgent: "Men of Galilee, why do you stand looking up toward heaven? This Jesus, who has been taken up from you into heaven, will come in the same way as you saw him go" (Acts 1:11). The implication of what this angel seems to be saying is: "And when he comes again, he better not catch you standing around just staring up and doing nothing!"

We respond with urgency when a baby falls into a well, or when someone has a heart attack! In an urgent situation, a late response is useless, any chance of doing something useful gone in an instant and lost forever! That's why we call it an *emergency*!

If his office is on fire, does the bishop say: "Don't bother me now; I first have to finish this mail"? If a home is in flames, does a father with children inside that home call the fire department half an hour later? When the firefighters get the call, do they say, "Fine, we'll be dropping by after our coffee break"? Do the firefighters and the father then huddle around, talking calmly about the outside chance that the children may get out on their own "if only we *keep cool*"?

Too often today, the Church and the People of God are a little too cool, forgetting Christ's warning, "Because you are lukewarm, and neither cold nor hot, I

The world is in darkness, and we have the mission of rolling back the stone to let the light of the Risen Christ shine forth.

am about to spit you out of my mouth" (Revelation 3:16). We don't seem to realize it is the Father's house that's on fire, with his own beloved children inside! It is not time for a quiet chat or just another workshop. The mission to evangelize is urgent! We are searching for the lost sheep of Christ, and there are wolves out there waiting to tear them apart. A roaring lion is on the prowl, looking for those he can devour. The world is in darkness, and we have the mission of rolling back the stone to let the light of the Risen Christ shine forth.

Without Jesus, millions and even billions will know only terror and darkness. Countless numbers have totally lost their way, and we are sent to lead them safely home. They can so easily die without ever coming to know their Heavenly Father, and his Son who died to save them from death, and the Holy Spirit who is their only source of holiness and power!

Jesus himself sends us to these endangered millions living in fear, "to open their eyes so that they may turn from darkness to light and from the power of Satan to God, so that they may receive forgiveness of sins and a place among those who are sanctified by faith in me" (Acts 26:18). The message we bring is one of hope and lasting joy. And the encouraging promise with which we are sent is this: "Whoever brings back a sinner from wandering will save the sinner's soul from death and will cover a multitude of sins" (James 5:20).

The first Christians had a strong sense of urgency: "Every day in the temple and at home they did not cease to teach and proclaim Jesus as the Messiah" (Acts 5:42). "Woe to me if I do not proclaim the gospel. . . . I am entrusted with a commission. . . . I have made myself a slave to all, so that I might win more. . . . I have become all things to all people, that I might by all means save some" (1 Corinthians 9:16-22).

The Church today is telling us that our task is urgent, calling for an energetic and quick response: "The urgency of the church's mission is obvious" (*Redemptoris Missio*, 3). "What moves me even more strongly to proclaim the urgency of missionary evangelization is the fact that it is the *primary* service which the Church can render to every individual and to all humanity in the modern world, a world which . . . seems to have lost its sense of ultimate realities and of existence itself" (2).

So, LET'S GO!

1. Lets Go with God: It was God who multiplied the descendants of Abraham like the sands of the sea. Like Abraham, we too look forward "to the city . . . whose architect and builder is God" (Hebrews 11:10).

Shoot for the stars, aim at the heights of holiness, and take as many as you can along for the ride

2. Let's Go with the Word: "Is not my word like fire, says the LORD, and like a hammer that breaks a rock in pieces" (Jer-emiah 23:29)?

3. Let's Go Together and without Competition: Praying together, the twelve Apostles experienced the first Pentecost, and the beginnings of worldwide evangelization. "Now the whole group of those who believed were of one heart and soul, and no one claimed private ownership of any possessions, but everything they owned was held in common. With great power the apostles gave their testimony to the resurrection of the Lord Jesus, and great grace was upon them all" (Acts 4:32-33).

4. Let's Go with Courage: "For I am not ashamed of the gospel; it is the power of God for salvation to everyone who has faith" (Romans 1:16).

5. And Let's Also Go with Urgency! We are proclaimers of Christ, heralds of salvation! "How beautiful upon the mountains are the feet of the messenger who announces peace, who brings good news, who announces salvation, who says to Zion, 'Your God reigns' " (Isaiah 52:7).

In ancient times, news was carried by heralds, trained runners who sometimes ran themselves to death to bring the news of victory as quickly as possible. "Like the cold of snow in the time of harvest are faithful messengers to those who send them; they refresh the spirit of their masters" (Proverbs 25:13).

We have very little time! Tens of thousands will die today without coming to know God the Father, Son and Holy Spirit. If we work with urgency, that number will lessen and the company of the saved will grow. Jesus sends us out into the highways and byways for the purpose of filling the Father's house with wedding guests. That, better than anything else, shows him that his Son has not died in vain.

So blast off! Shoot for the stars, aim at the heights of holiness, and take as many as you can along for the ride. I'll see you when we get there. And if you happen to bring along a greater crowd than me, I will only be delighted and far more importantly, so too will Jesus!

For now, go with urgency, or in the dynamic words of Pope John Paul II, "'Put out into the deep' for a catch" (*Novo Millennio Ineunte*, 1). There's a whole world waiting to be evangelized, waiting for you! Go, chosen heralds of Jesus Christ. Run to win! No one ever had a greater opportunity. No one ever carried better news: the good news that Jesus Christ is with us, loving, saving, freeing, and sanctifying us, and remaining with us until the *end of time*!

Together with him, we really can MOVE IT OUT! So, let's do it: AMEN. n

About the Author

Fr. Tom Forrest, a Redemptorist priest, was ordained in New York in 1954. For the first twenty-three years of his priesthood, he worked among the poor of the Caribbean. In 1971, he became involved in the Charismatic Renewal, and in 1978 was elected director of the International Office for Catholic Charismatic Renewal. He served in this capacity for six years, first with Cardinal Suenens in Brussels and then in Rome.

He has traveled to and spoken in more than 104 different countries, and his articles and books have been translated into a number of languages. He has organized two Worldwide Retreats for Priests, one in 1984 on the theme *A Call to Holiness*, and the other in 1990 on the theme *Called to Evangelize*. A total of 11,000 priests attended the retreats, which both took place in the Papal Audience Hall.

Fr. Forrest has worked at the Vatican Congregation for the Clergy, collaborating to promote annual events to foster priestly renewal. At present, he is International Director of Evangelization 2000, a Catholic effort to promote Church renewal through prayer, proclamation of the Word, and the formation of a more evangelistically activated people of God. He resides in Washington, D.C.